3. 5. 80

Creative Classroom

A Kathryn Shoemaker Craft Book

by Kathryn E. Shoemaker

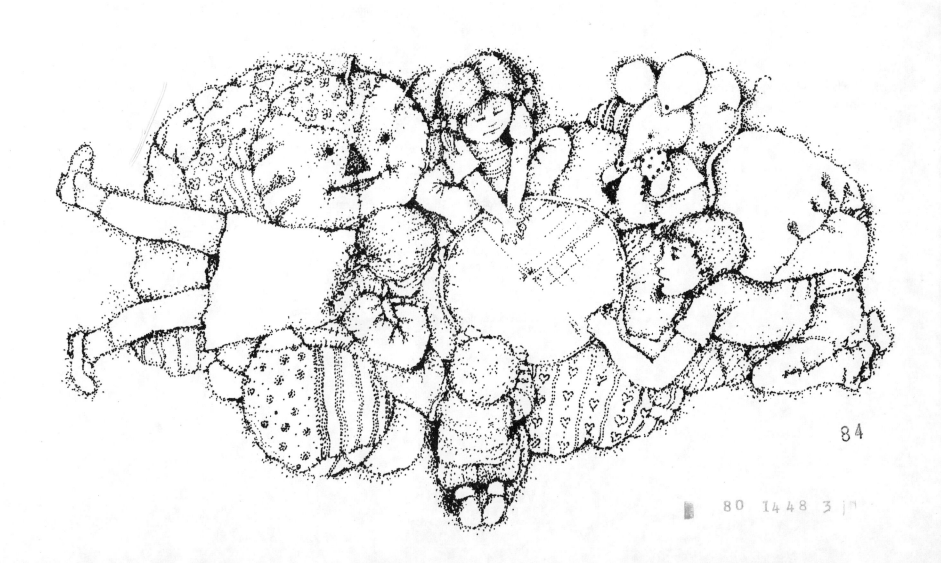

84

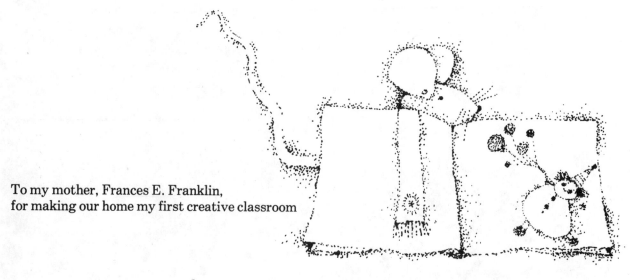

To my mother, Frances E. Franklin,
for making our home my first creative classroom

Other Books by the Author:
Listen to the Children (with Virginia Gaston)
Creative Christmas

Copyright © 1980 by Kathryn E. Shoemaker

Library of Congress Catalog Card Number: 79-64651
ISBN: 0-03-053441-0

Printed in the United States of America

5   4   3   2   1

Winston Press
430 Oak Grove
Minneapolis, Minnesota 55403

Dear Gentle Reader,

Twenty years ago, when my mother was a kindergarten teacher, she asked me to make figures for her flannelboard. For fifteen years before that, she had kept me supplied with paper, crayons, and paints, guarding against the intrusion of commercial coloring books. My first creative classroom—where this book really began—was the kitchen of our home. In that kitchen/classroom I did child's work—writing my own stories, drawing and painting my own pictures, and playing with the basic materials of our physical life: water, dirt, sand, food, fibers, and growing things. To make it a creative classroom, my mother did adult's work—giving structure to my life by providing the time and materials for my work and play and by protecting my natural curiosity from adult-imposed standards.

Later I was fortunate enough to have teachers who gave me the same kind of encouragement in their creative classrooms. In those wonderful classrooms, as the teachers read aloud, as I planned projects with other students, as I wrote stories, and even as I blew imaginary bubbles back and forth to other students, this book continued to grow.

More formally, this book began with that first flannelboard of my mother's. Later there were additional requests from my mother and from other teachers and a job designing learning materials and environments for a large public-school district.

The characteristics of a creative classroom have become clear to me through my own learning experiences as well as through my work with teachers and schools. Of course, the first and most obvious element is the teacher. The teacher makes the difference between a plain classroom and a creative one. The teacher makes the difference by enjoying, even loving, his or her work, providing an environment that gives children's creativity and curiosity a chance to grow.

Happily for me, I had teachers who loved to read aloud, as my mother did. Those who did not read aloud told stories to the class. I had teachers who loved paper, paint, and clay; they gave me time and freedom to draw, paint, and sculpt. Teachers who loved to sing and dance gave me encouragement in music and drama.

I hope that this collection of designs for a creative classroom will add new life and interest to familiar activities and materials. In designing these learning materials, I have tried to do enough planning to help those teachers who want to devote their time to reading, writing, or other activities—rather than working on the classroom itself. But I have also tried to leave some of the creativity in the hands of the teacher and the child.

In a creative classroom, one must do everything possible to protect and preserve the children's natural creativity and curiosity and to avoid imposing adult patterns or viewpoints on their young minds. The patterns in this

book are to be used by adults; I hope that no one will allow children to use these patterns for tracing, cutting, or coloring. Using patterns, like coloring in commercial coloring books, encourages staying in the lines or cutting straight rather than giving free rein to the imagination. Children's visual perceptions suffer when their creativity is stifled; this is never done intentionally but occurs when innocent incidents inflict cumulative damage. First, coloring books are offered to children whose natural inclination is to scribble, and coloring within the lines is rewarded. Instead of discovering forms in their own fanciful scribbling, children memorize prescribed shapes; they use adult formulas rather than their own universal ones, and they don't develop a personal creative viewpoint. Then, when they are asked to draw something new, they are not able to coordinate eyes, hands, and imagination.

These creative classroom ideas are for every kind of learning situation. They are for classroom teachers, Sunday-school teachers, scout leaders, club leaders, and parents—for anyone who needs some new lines for old tunes. The ideas are designed as much for the teacher's happiness as for the students' enjoyment. Happy, interested teachers motivate their students.

I hope you find something in this book that makes you want to gather up materials, to build, to write, or to plan a creative new strategy for your students. Perhaps you will find a handy timesaving hint or a solution to a problem. May whatever you find be a helpful addition to your already creative classroom.

Kathryn E. Shoemaker
Cambria, California

Table of Contents

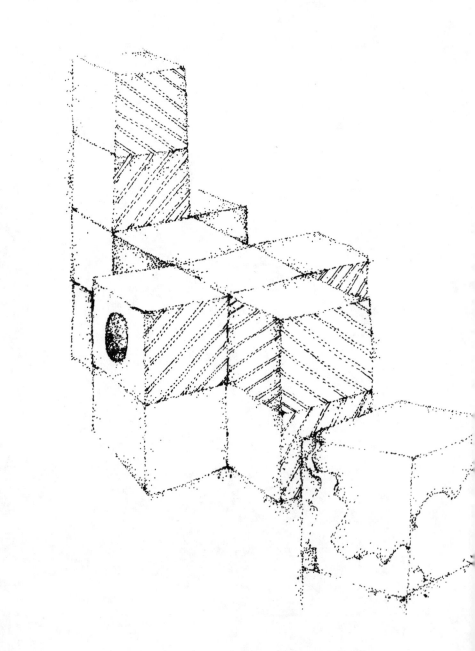

Children learn more in an interesting, well-designed learning environment, and they feel happier in pleasant, colorful rooms. Creating an interesting and colorful environment is the first step in designing a creative classroom.

Use the ideas in this chapter to make your room more interesting—to add color, to make new display areas, to solve storage problems imaginatively. Remember to leave some simple, restful spots in the room; too many fascinating displays and arrangements can overwhelm children, making it difficult for them to focus on an individual object.

Money is always a major consideration, so most of these ideas are simple and inexpensive. The more time you spend in planning your creative classroom, the more money you will save. When you involve students in creating the new environment themselves, you can save both time and money.

The suggestions in this chapter can help you to create an attractive, inviting classroom for your students. You can also use these ideas to decorate a child's bedroom, areas of your home or office, or community work or play spaces.

I have used most of the ideas in my own home and office. As a collector of all kinds of scraps and tidbits, I know that storing toys or special treasures is a problem in both the classroom and the home. By the time my daughter was three, she had acquired an enormous collection of purses from garage sales and thrift shops. To solve this particular storage problem, I covered a soundboard with cloth and nailed it to her bedroom wall. Then I attached thirty-five hooks to the board, and Kristie's collection of purses became an attractive and handy display. It was also much easier for me to find a purse to borrow when they were all off the floor and in clear view. The cloth-covered boxes described on page 5 have also solved many storage problems for me.

The Basics of a Children's Art Program

The most basic and important part of a children's art program is painting; children need to paint for painting's sake. They may paint with a purpose—making boxes, cardboard construction, papier-mâché decorations, cloth for scenery, and posters—but they need to paint just for the fun of it. From the time they are old enough to hold paint brushes, most children love to paint. With a patient, supervising adult, a one-year-old can start painting.

Tempera paint is universally appealing and versatile; it suits the painting style of young children more than watercolors, oils, or acrylics. To use tempera paint, you will need a few good, big brushes and paper or cardboard.

Easels are desirable, but you can always cover the floor or a table with newspapers and let the students paint on a flat surface. If you don't have other materials for them to paint, give children cardboard or wood scraps to paint on; cloth scraps and scraps of paper from a printing shop also work. Before children start to paint, explain why it's important to keep brushes in one color and to rinse them out so that the colors won't get muddy.

Mix a bit of liquid detergent with the paint and let children paint the windows of your room. This can be done all through the year, not just for special holidays. Paint the windows with valentines, kites, spring flowers, or with scenery that fits your social-studies or history unit.

Some children always want to paint, and others need motivation. For those who need motivation, read or tell a story, sing a song, or discuss something to get their imaginations going. Have them illustrate the story, paint the way the song makes them feel, or show the solution to a problem.

Once children have had experience painting with tempera, show them how to try more sophisticated tempera techniques. Thicken the basic paint with cornstarch, detergent, or sand, or add egg yolks. Use pen and ink to add touches to the tempera paintings. Look for books that demonstrate other tempera techniques. This activity will suggest interesting possibilities and encourage variety in their paintings.

In addition to painting, children need experience modeling with materials such as clay and playdough. Playdough can be made in a few minutes, but clay is more versatile. Both materials must be cared for so they won't dry up. Many teachers shy away from clay because they don't know how to handle or fire it. I feel it is important to give children experience working with clay even if you aren't used to working with it or firing it. Perhaps another teacher or a parent will help you to begin working with these materials.

Most children quickly figure out what to do with clay; they love to handle it and to see what can be done with it. At times clay brings out silliness in children who haven't had experience playing with messy materials. Sometimes those children need time to play with the clay in an immature way, mushing it into formless lumps. Eventually they tire of that and begin to play with the clay more constructively.

If the mess bothers you, have the children play with the clay in a small, controlled setting. Adult intervention should be restricted, but try to maintain a productive play atmosphere. Don't allow the clay to be thrown, splashed, or played with destructively. While supervising this activity, do not form anything out of the clay; children will invariably try to copy it, and in doing so they won't use their own creativity. Before children are ready to learn techniques from adults, such as throwing a pot on a wheel, they need to know how the clay feels in their hands, how it reacts to pressure from their fingertips, and how it acts when water is poured on it.

In your art program, use natural materials: water, sand, dirt, clay, food, and wood. Knowledge about these materials comes from playing with them. Children who have played with natural materials come to school filled with knowledge that helps their academic achievement. For example, in arithmetic, the concept of fractions is not nearly as difficult for a child who has played with wood blocks or divided a mud pie as it is for a child who hasn't had those experiences.

In planning your art program, keep in mind the goal of self-discovery. If children learn something on their own, they will remember it forever; if you tell them about it, they will probably forget. When children are given the time to play, they will find joy in self-discovery and be more willing to look for and try new things. That is the joy of learning.

Fabric Transformations

The fastest and most dramatic way to change a room is to cover as much of it as you can with fabric. In a few hours, with a standard desk stapler, you can change an ordinary, even an ugly, room into a beautiful one.

Materials:
- fabric
- stapler

To begin the fabric transformation, cut your fabric 2-3″ longer and wider than the wall space to be covered. Staple the fabric along the top first, turning the edges under as you go and pulling it gently, but firmly, to remove wrinkles. If the fabric is creased, iron it first. Leave perfectionism behind; the purpose of this activity is to brighten the room quickly. In a large room, imperfections won't be noticeable. Don't be afraid to begin; if your work turns out poorly, pull the fabric off and start over.

Look for fabric at discount stores. Burlap is inexpensive, but it fades quickly and looks worn. Felt is the best long-term purchase; it costs more than cottons and polyesters, but it lasts forever and makes a good surface for pinning. A wall covered with felt becomes a giant flannelboard and improves the room's acoustics. Felt comes in 72″ widths and is reusable. Muslin is another inexpensive choice, and it can be dyed any color. Irregular bedsheets on sale are the best buy per yard, and they can also be dyed. At thrift shops and garage sales, look for plain sheets, curtains, or fabric remnants. Look for large-size dresses too. Some dresses may have enough material to cover a sizable bulletin board or wall. You can also cut the dresses into strips and squares and combine them to make a patchwork bulletin board or small patchwork hangings. In selecting fabric, choose colors you can live with. Imagine or hold up assorted holiday color

combinations against the fabrics. Choose the fabric that looks best with several different colors.

Look around your classroom for other surfaces that can be improved with bright fabric—dirty, worn cupboards, the backs of freestanding bookshelves, even scratched and battered wood surfaces. Put fabric around the room on tabletops and windows.

Cloth-Covered Panels

If you have brick or concrete walls in the classroom and can't staple fabric directly onto them, you can cover panels of unpainted soundboard or acoustic board with fabric. The panels are 4' x 8' and ½" thick; lumberyards will cut them to fit your specifications. (Avoid wall board; it is heavier and too hard for inserting pins or staples.) You'll need three yards of 54" fabric to cover each 4' x 8' board. Cut the fabric 2" longer and 2" wider than the board, piecing it if you need to. Place the board on a large table and lay the fabric on it, smoothing away the wrinkles and distributing the cloth evenly. Pin the fabric to the underside of the board, inserting a pin every 5" to hold the cloth in place. Then begin to staple the fabric to the back of the board, removing the pins and pulling the fabric firmly, but gently, to remove any wrinkles.

Large sheets of 1-2" styrofoam or corrugated cardboard have the advantage of being lightweight; they can be hung from ceilings or nailed or screwed to walls. For an instant art gallery, cover both sides of these styrofoam or cardboard panels with fabric and hang five to ten of them in a series of free-hanging rows. Pin the fabric to the styrofoam instead of stapling it. Staple fabric to the cardboard panels in the same way you would staple it to soundboard, or paint it with enamel or latex paint.

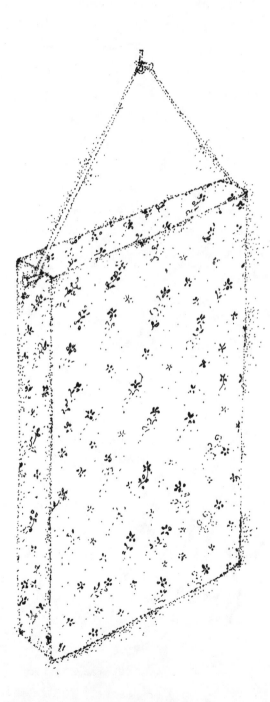

Cloth-Covered Boxes

Boxes can be used for puppet stages, playhouses, play furniture, giant life-size paper dolls, life-size animals, gameboards, bean-bag tosses, feely boxes, and supply centers. They can also solve most of your storage and space problems.

Purchase boxes at an appliance shop or look in the yellow pages for cardboard-box manufacturers. Boxes can be ordered in white or brown and in the exact size you want; to get the best price, order in quantity. Boxes of the same size stack and store more easily; 12" and 16" cubes are the most practical and versatile.

Materials:
- boxes
- fabric
- bowl
- white latex glue, water, and a brush
- scissors, pencil, ruler, pins, tape, stapler

To staple fabric on a 12" box, cut one 13" x 49" strip and two 13" squares of fabric. Turn one end of the long strip under ½". Wrap the strip around the box, pinning the turned end over the other end. Then pin the top and bottom edges of the strip onto the top and bottom of the box, making a fold at each corner so the cloth will lie flat. Staple the fabric in place, removing the pins. Now turn in the edges of the 13" squares ½". Pin and staple the squares onto the exposed sides of the box, covering the overhang from the stapled strip. For variety, cut six smaller squares in assorted fabrics and staple them to the box using the same method.

It is more work to glue fabric onto boxes, but glue strengthens the boxes and the fabric is less likely to be pulled off. Mix one part water and one part glue in a bowl. Cut two squares and one long strip of fabric, as you did

1. Draw basic shape on a large box.

2. Cut away ends and small windows.

3. Paint boat shape.
   Paint waves and ladder.

in the stapling method. Working on a protected surface, brush glue onto the fabric until it is totally covered. Wrap the glued strip around the box, pressing the fabric down and turning the box as you go; leave a ½″ overhang on both sides. Then press the overhang down onto the top and bottom of the box, making a little tuck in each corner. Turn in ½″ around the edges of the 13″ squares and glue them to the uncovered sides of the box. If the fabric pops up, pin it down until the glue dries. Allow the fabric to dry completely before using the box.

Instead of using fabric, you can quickly cover boxes with almost any kind of paint. For easy care and durability, enamel paint is best. One coat of paint will cover white boxes; two coats are needed for brown boxes. To save on enamel paint, prime the box with a coat of white paint.

To cover boxes with contact paper, cut the paper 2″ wider than the perimeter of your box. Start to pull the paper away from its backing. Then press the edge of the exposed paper along the edge of one side, pressing lightly in case you have to lift the paper to adjust the fit. Hold each side of the backing and pull gently. Stop pulling and press the newly exposed section of contact paper onto the box, gently smoothing away wrinkles and overlapping the ends of the strip. Then make two squares and use the same method to apply them to the top and bottom of the box.

Covering Other Containers

If you can cover a box with cloth, you can cover a can. Ask a local ice-cream store to save large containers for you, ask the school cafeteria for one-gallon cans, and save your own three-pound coffee cans. To cover a metal can, tape a strip of lightweight cardboard around it and glue the fabric to the cardboard.

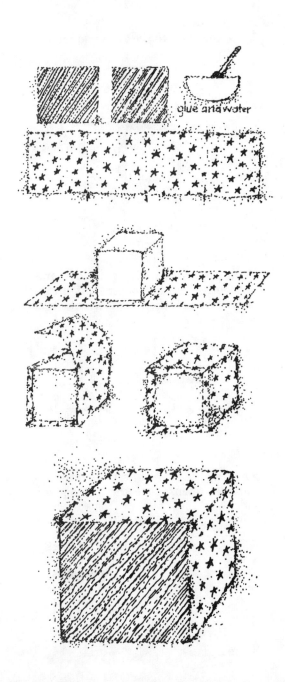

Enamel paint or contact paper can be applied directly to metal cans. You can also draw, paint, or collage words and pictures onto construction-paper strips, cover the strips with clear contact paper or laminating film, and tape them on cans. Putting holiday gifts in cans has become an official enterprise in shopping centers. For pennies, you can make your own gift cans.

Once you begin to look for cans, you'll see that large cottage cheese and yogurt cartons are good storage containers. Even ordinary egg cartons have a variety of storage uses in the classroom. They are terrific for sorting buttons and beads or for individual sewing kits with cups for pins, buttons, needles, thread, and scissors. To cover these kinds of cartons, glue fabric onto them or cover them with contact paper. Then put samples of their contents on the containers—put macaroni on a macaroni container or wrap a can with yarn and put balls of embroidery yarn in it.

Custom-Made Boxes

If you can't find or buy a container to suit your needs, you can make one in the exact shape, size, and color you want.

Materials:
- cardboard or chipboard
- masking tape
- ruler, pencil
- heavy-duty knife or paper cutter that will cut cardboard or chipboard
- paint, fabric, or contact paper

To make a 12″ cube, cut six 12″ squares of cardboard.

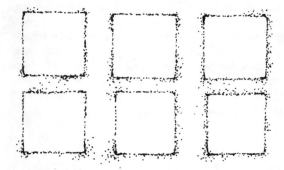

Place one square in the center of the table and arrange four squares around it so that one side of each square is aligned 1/8″ from the center square, as shown.

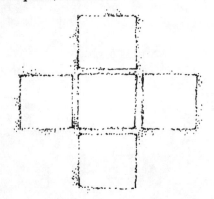

Tape each side to the center square.

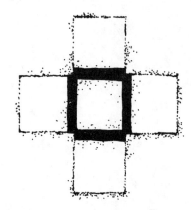

Then lift up two adjacent sides and tape them together at the corner. Lift up another two sides and tape them together at the corner.

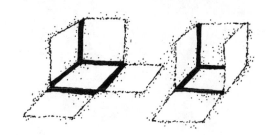

Now tape the two untaped corners. For a flat lid that opens, tape the last square onto one side.

If you want a hole in the top of the box, cut the hole first and then tape the top to all four sides; make the hole large enough for your hand to fit through the opening. Paint the box with a coat of latex paint and a second coat of enamel, or cover it with fabric or contact paper.

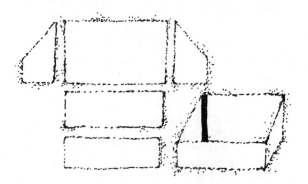

Once you've made a basic box, you can make up your own size and shape specifications for additional boxes. For the file box, the front and back sections are the same width but different heights. The base is the same width as the front and back sections and the same length as the side sections. Follow the diagram, taping the pieces together and covering the box the same way you taped and covered the 12″ cube.

Frames

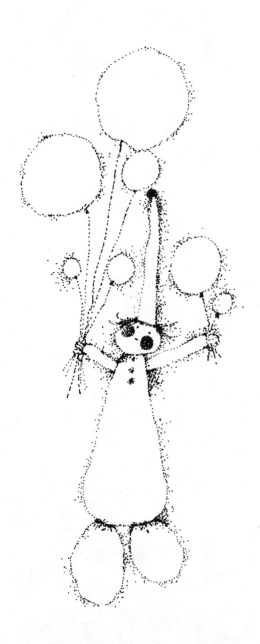

What you do with children's art influences them more than what you say to them about it. Your active appreciation helps children enjoy and value their own work. If adults display their art, children retain a sense of pride in it.

When I was a child, my mother displayed my art work. We lived in a small apartment, and she put my work up in its tiny kitchen. One day she taped up a clown I had made, a clown who was holding a bunch of balloons. Some time later, while she was busy, I decided to "complete the picture" by drawing balloons all over the kitchen. I drew clusters of balloons on every cupboard, drawer, and wall, like a wallpaper pattern. I wish I could remember my mother's expression—it must have been one of masked horror. I do remember cleaning the crayon off the walls and the cupboards, but I don't remember receiving any kind of punishment. Although my judgment was questionable, I think the fact I felt confident enough of my work to attempt to redecorate the kitchen is to my mother's credit. Through her appreciation of my art work, she had nurtured a sense of power in me, a sense that I could change myself and my environment in positive ways. If my clown looked good, why not more balloons? (I hope I'm not discouraging anyone from displaying children's work for fear that the walls and cupboards will be lavished with dancing purple cows or fancy rocketships.)

Many books on children's art stress the importance of displaying the art formally in carefully cut frames. This is probably the nicest way, but how many classroom teachers have the time to fit framemaking into the many other things they have to do? It's much better to pin up a picture hastily than not to display it at all. However, if you have time, prepare some frames and have them on hand.

Here are some suggestions for making frames. Make an assortment of construction-paper frames in a variety of colors. Cut two pieces of construction paper in the same size and shape. Then cut a frame opening in one of the pieces and tape the two pieces together on three sides using cloth mystic-tape. Then slide a picture into the frame.

For sturdier, longer lasting frames, use railroad board, lightweight cardboard, or mat board, the colored textured board that professionals use. Make these frames in the same way as the construction-paper frames, but before taping the two pieces together, tape a piece of clear plastic or mylar plastic over the inside of the opening.

Instead of cutting only rectangular frames, cut frames with circular, square, oval, and triangular openings in them. Make sets of frames that go together, for example, two brown mats, one with a square opening and a smaller one with a circular opening. Make three to five frames and choose new pictures for them every day, twice a week, or weekly. Ask the children to select some of the pictures for display and select some of them yourself, giving encouragement by showing the work of less confident children. Discuss the pictures with the class and ask children to describe the things that they like in the framed pictures.

Buy plastic-frame boxes from an art shop, or look for cheaper versions in dime stores or wholesale art warehouses. Plastic-frame boxes come in a complete range of sizes from 3″ x 5″ to 18″ x 24″. The following mylar-plastic pockets are easy-to-make substitutes for plastic-frame boxes.

Mylar-Plastic Pockets

Materials:
- mylar plastic
- clear, strong tape
- lightweight white cardboard

Cut a 20″ x 30″ piece of cardboard and a 20″ x 30″ sheet of mylar plastic. Place the mylar on top of the cut cardboard, matching the edges. With clear tape, tape three sides, as shown. Slip children's art work into the mylar pocket and pin the pocket to the wall, or lean it against the wall.

Variations

A picture kiosk is another way to display children's art. Get a large cardboard tube from a milk-carton or carpet company, or make your own tube out of a large appliance box. Cover it with paint or cloth and pin pictures on it.

Cardboard display easels are simple to make and are another good way to display children's art. Cut two sheets of cardboard into the same shapes, as shown, making them any size. Tape the two identical shapes together to form a freestanding easel.

Children's art can also be displayed on the room dividers or on stacks of decorated boxes described in the displays section of this chapter. Another way to display art work is to put up a clothesline and use clothespins to hang the pictures from it.

You can always pin or tape a collection of children's paintings on the wall. There's no faster way to transform a dull room than to put up the paintings of thirty-five kindergarten students. Make a solid wall of paintings, or put them up around the top of each wall, forming a border.

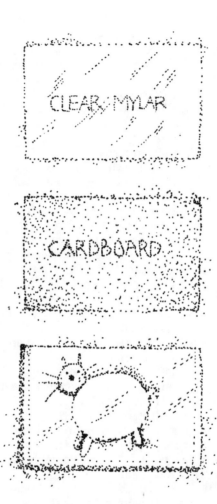

It's a good contrast for children to see their work displayed in a variety of ways. When they see their pictures displayed as posters and then in special frames, they learn that there are different ways to change their environment with art.

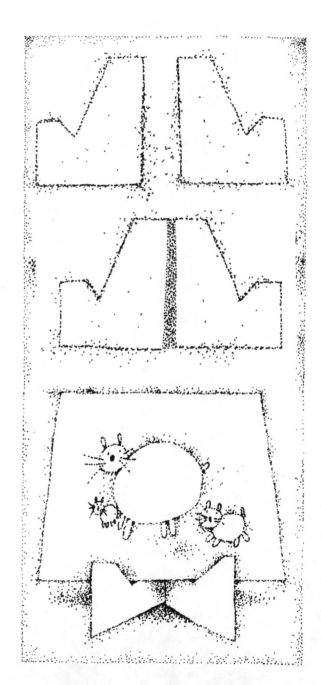

Giant Caterpillar Couch

Materials:
- large cloth scraps (sheets, large-size dresses, towels)
- pins, needles, thread
- sewing machine
- stuffing (old stockings, cloth, or polyester fill—if you can get it free or inexpensively)
- newspapers, pencils, scissors
- velcro or heavy-duty snaps

Before starting this project, enlist at least one volunteer parent or older student to operate the sewing machine. You may want to have several helpers, one to work with each child or with each pair of children. Each child can make a section of the caterpillar, or two children can work together on one section. Use the following steps, demonstrating each one first and then working with the children.

On a sheet of newspaper, draw and cut out a pattern for one pillow section (one pillow side).

Pin the pattern to a piece of fabric and cut it out. Do the same with a second piece of fabric.

For a crazy-quilt design, pin small pieces of fabric together to make one large piece. Then sew the small pieces together by hand, using a blanket stitch. Put the pattern on the large piece of fabric and cut it out.

Pin the two sections of the pillow together, matching right sides of the fabric, and use the sewing machine to stitch around the outside edges, about ½″ to 1″ from the edge of the fabric. Leave a 10″ opening for adding the stuffing.

Sew a strip of velcro or a set of snaps along both sides of the pillow, making sure that each pillow has the same amount of velcro or the same number of snaps so that the pillows will snap together easily.

Stuff the pillows and then sew up the openings by hand, using a slipstitch. Snap the caterpillar sections together.

To make the caterpillar's head, sew some eyes and feelers onto one end of the couch.

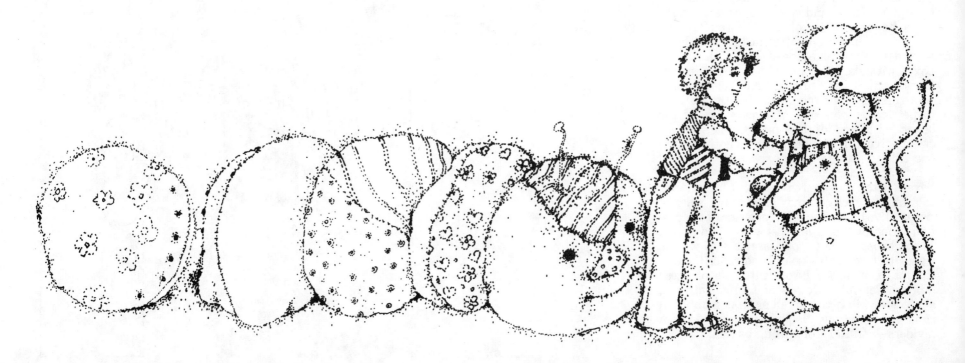

Displays

Make display spaces and room dividers from large sheets of cardboard or from cardboard boxes. To form a freestanding display unit with eight display sides, cut two 2' x 3' sheets of cardboard from a refrigerator box. Then paint the sheets with a base coat of latex paint. Make a slit in the center of each sheet, from the midpoint down, and slide the two sheets together, as shown. If you want larger sheets of cardboard, for example 5' x 5', order them from a cardboard-box manufacturer.

A collection of smaller boxes can be covered and used for both storage and display. Assemble 100 12″ cubes and paint or cover them, making each side of each cube a different color or pattern. For example, paint one side of each of the 100 boxes white and one side green. For the third side, choose three different Christmas prints—fabric or Christmas wrapping paper—and cover one side of thirty of the boxes with one of the Christmas prints, one side of thirty-five different boxes with the second print, and one side of the last thirty-five boxes with the third print. Next, choose four fabric or paper prints that compliment something in your room, such as the walls or carpet; cover one side of twenty-five of the boxes with one of the prints, one side of twenty-five different boxes with another print, one side of twenty-five boxes with the third print, and one side of the last twenty-five boxes with the fourth print. Choose four coordinated colors and paint one side of twenty-five boxes one color, one side of twenty-five different boxes another color, and so on. Then choose three to four fabrics that will go well with the painted colors and cover the last side of each of the boxes with one of these fabrics. Careful selection of fabric, patterns, and colors will give you an endless number of choices in forming display spaces and room dividers—and 100 storage bins as well!

Puppet Play

1. Choose a play starter.
2. Choose the puppets or patterns you will need.
3. Read the instructions on backs of the puppet patterns. Make your puppets.
4. Borrow the puppet stage.
5. Practice your play two times.
6. Invite some people to watch your puppet play.
7. Perform your play!

PUPPET PATTERNS

SEWING SUPPLIES

FELT SCRAPS

PLAY STARTERS

One Dark Night

One dark night... a funny fat chicken walked home through a forest. Fat chicken ran fast. She was scared. She was scared of the dark. She was scared of the tall trees. She was scared of the sound of the wind through the trees. Suddenly, a large... dropped out of the trees and... onto the scared chicken's head. Then she...

In learning centers, children work individually or in small groups without supervision, using mastered skills to explore and make discoveries. As a follow-up to a lesson, children may be assigned to work in a learning center, or they may work in it by choice. Learning centers are not a new concept; only their name is modern. For years teachers have used interest centers, work areas, bulletin boards, and bookshelves in much the same way we use learning centers today. When children are involved in organized, independent study or work, teachers have more time for individual and small-group instruction.

Learning centers take time and space to run. Each learning center is located in a specific area of the room and has its own sets of written or visual instructions and specific, organized materials. You may want to start with one center and gradually work up to four or five. Eventually you may have twenty or more learning centers, but this will happen only after the students have learned how to use the centers.

Design the first learning center around something that the students are already familiar with, such as making collages, so that the focus will be on learning how to use the center. Once students have mastered working in the first center, set up an additional center to give them a chance to practice and experiment with new subjects. Activities in the centers should reinforce what students know already and should challenge them to go beyond what they have learned in class.

The learning centers described in this chapter are primarily designed for tasks in the language arts. However, the basic ideas are adaptable to many other content areas. Specific tasks are given for some of the learning centers. Once children complete the suggested tasks they should be encouraged to go on to develop their own ideas.

Libraries have excellent books about learning centers, describing how to prepare activities and how to write task cards. Exchanging learning-center ideas with fellow teachers is also a good way to spark new ideas. Involve students in the centers by assigning them the job of keeping the centers stocked with paper, pencils, pens, or other materials.

Scout leaders, Sunday-school teachers, counselors, and parents can use learning centers too. Anyone who works with children can find a use for a learning center—what parent doesn't need a rainy-day center? And a homemade collage center will outlast many of today's fancy toys, including dolls who get rashes or have heart palpitations! Parents can create variations of any of the centers to suit their children's interests. A scout leader might set up a knot-tying center, or a Sunday-school teacher might create a printing center where children can print Bible verses.

You can make a learning center by pushing a desk or table against a bulletin board. Make a portable center out of a box, a file folder, a painting easel, a study carrel, a bookshelf, a desk, or the inside of a large appliance box. Following are plans for a number of portable centers. They are easy to store and transport and easy to set up anywhere or anytime.

Materials:
- cardboard boxes, cardboard, chipboard, or cans
- contact paper, fabric, wallpaper, or paint
- masking tape and cloth mystic-tape
- mat knife or X-acto knife
- stamp sets for printing task cards (see page 32), plastic peel-off letters, or letter stencils
- clear contact paper or laminating film
- metal rings of different sizes

Basic Designs for a Learning Center

Use these basic designs to hold the materials and instructions for the projects learned in each center.

Box Design

Cut a hole in one side of the box so students can reach inside to take out materials for their projects. On one side of the box write the instructions for the primary task to be learned in this center. Make a pocket out of paper or acetate, and glue or tape it to a third side; variations on the projects can be slipped into the pocket and remain visible. Decorate the fourth side in any way you'd like.

Easel Design

Easel centers can be placed on a table and used by two students at the same time. Cut two 15″ x 24″ pieces of board and one 24″ x 12″ piece. Cover each of the boards with contact paper, fabric, or enamel paint. Punch two holes in each 15″ x 24″ board, 1″ from the top and 1-2″ from each side. Tape the two 24″ x 15″ pieces together as shown. Tape the 12″ x 24″ strip to one 24″ x 15″ piece; tape the 24″ sides together, leaving ¼″ between the two pieces so that the sides will bend easily. Insert metal rings in the holes and use them to hold task cards and charts.

Make variations of this easel design by using boards large enough to accommodate two or three sets of task cards as shown, or by varying the overall size of the easel for use with small index cards or with large sheets of chart paper.

Multisided Folding Design

Cut two to six 12″ x 15″ pieces of cardboard. Cover them with cloth or contact paper and tape them together as shown.

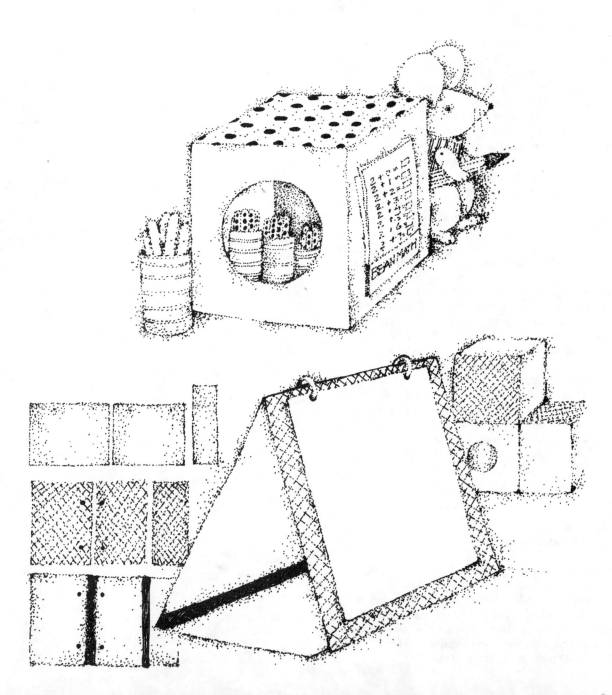

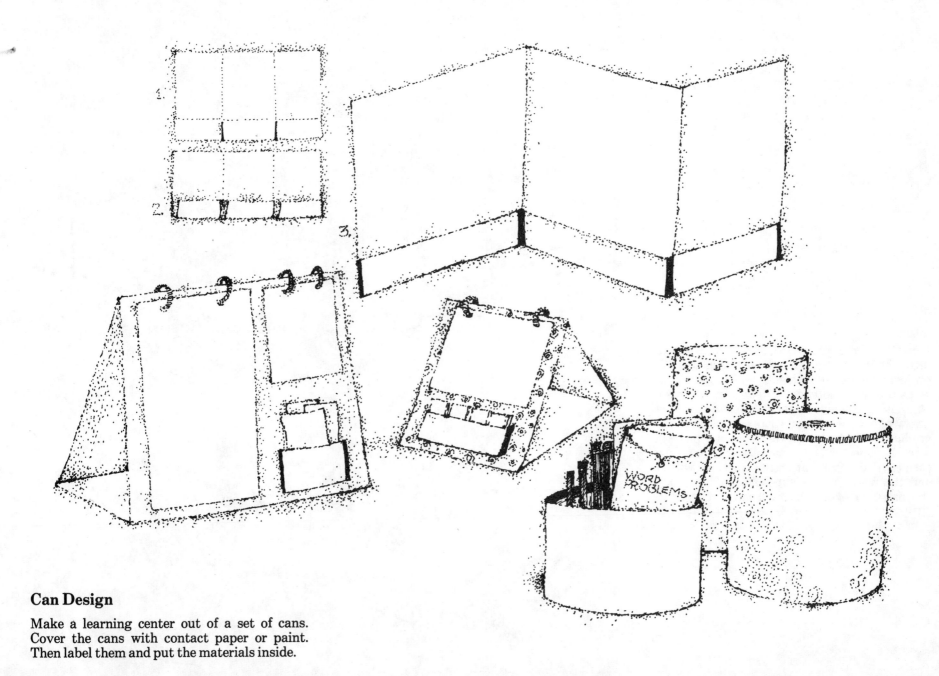

Can Design

Make a learning center out of a set of cans.
Cover the cans with contact paper or paint.
Then label them and put the materials inside.

Task Cards and Charts

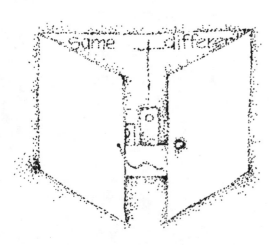

After you construct a basic center, write or print the instructions for the learning center's projects clearly and attractively on task cards or charts. Use notebook paper if you have a laminating machine; otherwise use tagboard or heavy paper. Before you write on the task card or chart, sketch the instructions on a piece of scratch paper in the same size as your final card to make sure that the instructions will fit and the words are evenly spaced. Then copy the instructions onto the task card or chart.

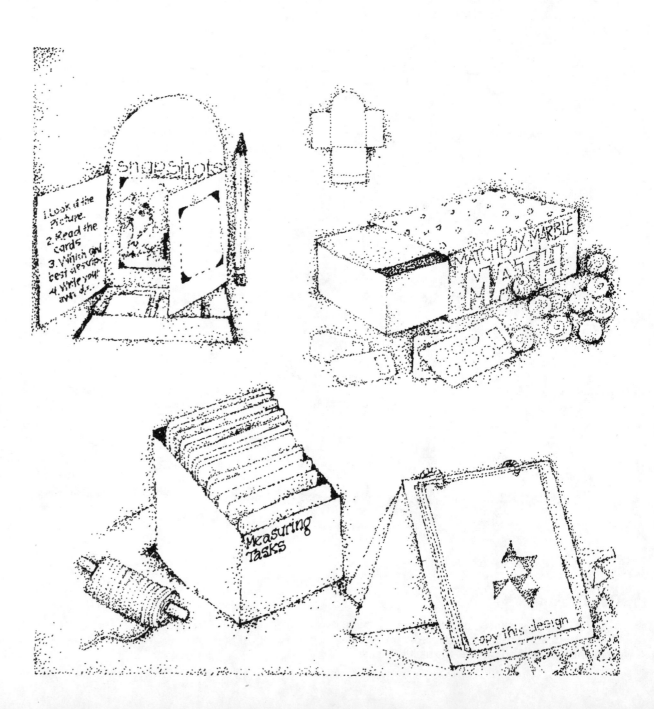

1. Place this pattern on a sheet of tissue paper.
2. Trace around the pattern. Cut it out.
3. Pin the tissue pattern onto a doubled piece of cloth.
4. Cut it out. Pin both pieces together.
5. Stitch "½" around the edge as indicated by the dotted lines.

(turn over)

snail stories

counting caterpiller tasks

Dial-a-Collage Center

In this center, students spin a dial to choose a collage-starter task card. This card gives them directions to pick out the boxes of collage materials they will use in their projects.

Materials:
- cardboard
- food cartons or boxes
- masking tape or glue
- marking pen
- collage materials
- compass
- paper fasteners
- spinners
- collage-starter task cards
- box

Cut three 18″ x 12″ pieces of cardboard. Then cut six food cartons or boxes in half. If you cannot obtain any cartons or boxes, make twelve boxes of your own. For each box, cut one 5″ x 3″ piece of cardboard, one 5″ x 2″ piece, and two 2″ x 3″ pieces. Tape the four pieces together as shown on page 8. Tape or glue the halved containers onto two of the 18″ x 12″ pieces of cardboard and number them from 1 to 12. Put different collage materials in each box.

Use a compass to draw a 10″ circle on the third 18″ x 12″ piece of cardboard. Print the numbers 1 to 12 evenly spaced around the outside of the circle. Poke a hole in the center of the circle and use a paper fastener to attach a spinner: this is your dial. Make several collage-starter task cards and put them in a box next to the dial.

Collage-Starter Task Cards

Here are some sample directions to write on the task cards. There are five numbered directions, one for each card. Be sure to print them clearly so that the students can read them without your help.

1. Spin the dial two times. Go to the two boxes with these numbers and choose a few items from each box. Use them to make a repeating design.

2. Spin the dial three times. Go to the three boxes with these numbers and choose a few items from each box. Use them to make a circular design. First, put a dot in the middle of a 12″ x 12″ square. Use your collage items to make circles around the dot. Sometimes use the same items in each circle; other times use two or three different items in each circle to make a pattern.

3. Spin the dial four times. Go to the four boxes with these numbers and choose a few items from each box. Use them to decorate the edges of a piece of paper. Write a letter to a friend on your paper.

4. Spin the dial eight times. Go to the eight boxes with these numbers and choose a few items from each box. Then cut out two cardboard circles. Slit each circle halfway to the center and then slip the circles together. Glue a different collage item on each part of your two circles.

5. Spin the dial three times. Go to the three boxes with these numbers and choose a few items from each box. Then cut out a paper, a cloth, and a cardboard square, all in the same size. Glue a different collage item on each piece to make a design.

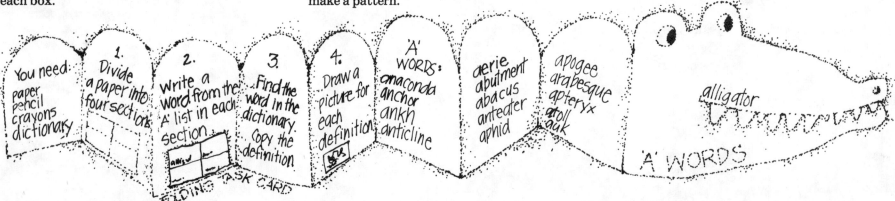

Collage Centers

Give children a dish of glue, a box of paper and cloth scraps, and something to stick the scraps on and you will see how much children love to collage. Everyone can cut, tear, and paste. Since drawing skill is not required, it's an easy craft for people to try. Older people do collage and call it "montage," "decoupage," "appliqué," and "assemblage." Children call collage "cut and paste." Whatever it's called, this activity seems to be universally interesting. Results will vary with age, concentration, and skill.

A Basic Collage Center

Use nine 12″ cardboard boxes with a hole cut in one side of each box. Each box will hold one type of collage item. Stack the boxes into three rows of three boxes. On top of the boxes place a flat box containing glue, scissors, plastic trays, and egg cartons holding a selection of collage items chosen from the nine boxes. Children can select items from this box when the larger stacked boxes are being used by someone else. To label each of the nine stacked boxes, glue a sample collage item on the box as shown. Put several plastic tubs or small, cut-down milk cartons in each box; use these tubs or cartons to hold the collage items.

Variation

Make a giant version of the center out of twenty-four 12″ cubes and arrange them in a three-foot cube.

Collage Trays

Find a set of 3″ or 4″ high boxes with lids. Make one following the directions on page 8, or get boxes from a supermarket or liquor store, cut them down to 4″ with an X-acto knife or sharp kitchen knife, and make lids out of the extra cardboard.

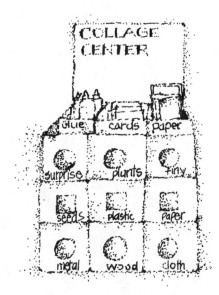

Use collage trays to make small collage centers. If you don't have much space in your classroom, these trays make a collage center that is more convenient than a center made of stacked boxes. Each tray can contain a selection of items to collage, a bottle of glue, scissors, and a pen. One tray can contain different types of pasta and another can hold things made of fiber, weaving samples, stitchery, or special ribbons. A third tray can hold a selection of seed pods, dried plants, leaves, and other natural items.

Here is a list of things to put into a collage box, collage tray, or collage center.

- new or used envelopes, some with windows
- new or used stamps
- stickers
- full-color mail-order catalogs
- gift-wrapping paper
- assorted paper scraps
- any kind of food wrappers
- old photos, postcards, cards, and letters
- box tops, can labels, newspapers
- comics, old books, magazines
- cloth and yarn scraps
- dried rice or beans
- leaves, dirt, sand, gravel, pebbles
- dried plants
- pasta in all shapes and sizes
- straws cut into shorter pieces
- buttons, beads, costume jewelry
- wood scraps, wood turnings, spools
- styrofoam packing fillers

Note: It is always important to use good sense in preparing collage activities for very small children. Children under three should be closely supervised and only given things that are too big to swallow. A two-year-old cannot be expected to do a bean collage alone without being tempted to stick a bean in his or her mouth or nose.

The Monster Maker

Students spin dials to find out the color and number of arms, legs, heads, and other body parts to draw on their monsters.

Once the monsters are made, they can be used to create any number of learning aids that will help children master math facts, word skills, foreign languages, science facts, or grammar. (See chapter 3 for learning-aid ideas.)

Materials:
- cardboard
- compass
- colored marking pens
- scissors
- paper fasteners
- spinners
- scratch paper
- construction paper or lightweight cardboard

On a large piece of cardboard draw four large circles. Divide the first circle into sections and write the name of a body part in each section: *arms, legs, head, eyes, nose, mouth, fingers, teeth, tail, wig, antennae, scales, fins, fur, skin.* Divide the second circle into ten sections and number them 1 to 10. Divide the third circle into several sections and color each one, writing the name of the color in each section. Divide the fourth circle into sections and write descriptive adjectives in each one: *rough, smooth, rippled, wrinkled, spiked, horny, quilled, slimy, bumpy.* If you make the circles on laminated cardboard and write on them with water-soluble pens or grease pencils, you will be able to wipe off the words and write different ones in their place. Punch a hole in the center of each circle and use a paper fastener to attach a spinner to each one.

Try this activity out yourself before asking students to make their own monsters. To start the activity, take out paper and a pencil. Spin the first circle. If the spinner stops at the word

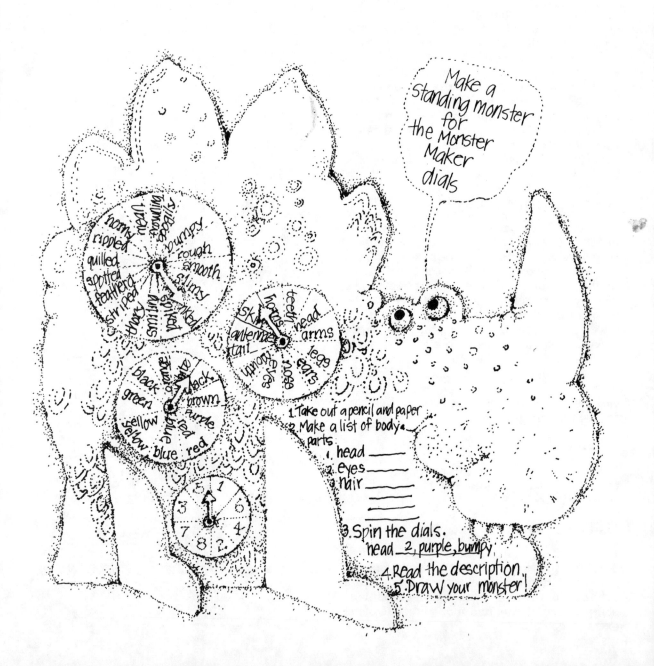

head, for example, write *head* on your paper. Now spin the dial on the second, third, and fourth circles and write down the information you get, for example, *3, brown, scaly*. Spin the dials three more times for each circle until you have a list of body parts, numbers, colors, and adjectives such as the following: *head, 3, brown, scaly; arms, 4, green, furry; eyes, 1, red, bumpy; fingers, 1, yellow, scaly*. Set a limit on the number of spins. The four spins above give a good description. Now draw your monster on scratch paper, drawing in the numbers of parts you have dialed and making up the rest of the monster's body. Then cut out your drawing and trace it on a sheet of construction paper or lightweight cardboard. Cut out the tracing and draw and color in the details using the colors you dialed.

To use the monsters as math pencil-pokes, have the students punch holes with a pencil at 1″ intervals around the outside edges of their monsters. On the front of the monster, write a math fact, such as 5 x 5, next to each hole. On the back, write the answer (25) next to the same holes. Make a monster for each times table or for sets of addition, subtraction, or division facts. Each child could make his or her own set of arithmetic pencil pokes, or the students can cooperate on one complete set for the whole class. If everyone in the class is going to use the same set, laminate the monsters or cover them with clear contact paper.

The monster maker can also be used as a story starter by having students make characters for the stories. You might add a superhero maker and have students make heroes who can have adventures with the monsters; make the same kind of dials but write in details about superheroes. The variations are countless. Children may come up with creature makers of their own.

MAGIC CASTLE

STORY STARTERS

1. Choose a can.
2. Read the instructions
3. Practice the technique
4. Choose a Story starter
5. Sketch your story
6. Use the new technique to illustrate your story.

The Magic Castle

This is a center for learning a variety of illustration techniques. Use the techniques for fun activities or for illustrating student-written stories and books. Children should learn and practice the techniques before using them to illustrate a story.

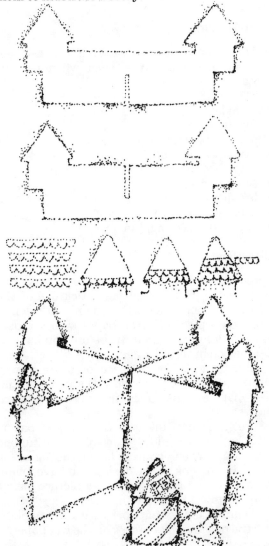

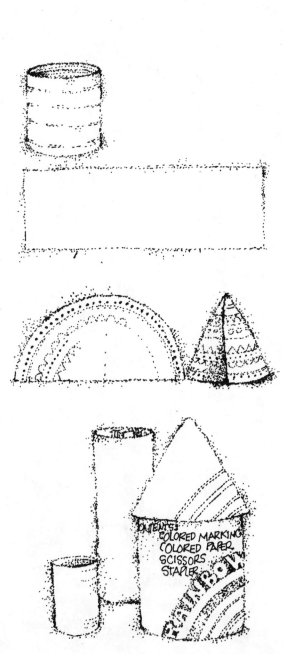

When you first introduce this center, you may want to use only two to three cans of techniques. Add more techniques when the first ones are mastered. If one technique is popular, make several cans of it so that more students can work at the same time. This center is adaptable to individual desk work. Children can check out a can, take it to their desks, and return it when the project is finished.

Materials:
- 3-lb. cans
- construction paper
- transparent tape
- clear contact paper
- bits of paper
- colored marking pens
- toothpicks or thin dowels

Decorate a can for each illustration technique you want to include. To cover each can, cut a strip of construction paper that is the same height as the can and long enough to encircle it; you may have to tape two pieces of paper together. Then decorate the strip with torn paper, or use colored marking pens to draw colorful decorations. You can also use the illustration technique to decorate the can. Make a list of the materials contained in the can and write it on the outside.

On another piece of colored paper make a flag and attach it to a toothpick or dowel. Write the name of the illustration technique, for example *Pencil, Pencil,* on the flag. Attach the flag to the can as a label for the activity.

In each can, put the basic materials required for the technique, a laminated card with easy-to-follow directions, a few drawing starters, and several samples of the technique done by other students. Stack the cans, circle them around a cardboard base, or place them on a box. Put a box with an assortment of papers next to or in the middle of the castle of cans.

Here are directions for the illustration techniques that students will use in the magic castle. Write these directions on laminated cards and place them in the illustration-technique cans. You may want to make up your own titles for these techniques.

Pencil, Pencil

Pencils are ordinary items, but they can be used with sensitivity and skill to create delicate drawings.

Materials:
- drawing pencils
- hand-size pencil sharpener
- small pieces of paper
- sandpaper

Directions

Sharpen your pencil and then make it sharper by rubbing the side of the lead back and forth against the sandpaper. On a piece of scrap paper, start a zigzag by rubbing the side of the pencil point on the paper. Continue to zigzag without removing the pencil from the paper. Make rows of tiny and large zigzags. Start one row with dark zigzags and gradually make the zigzags lighter until the pencil lines disappear altogether. Zigzag in one direction; then reverse and slant the pencil lines in another direction. Draw a whole picture using only zigzags and without lifting your pencil off the paper.

Pencil and Fingers Together

Directions

Draw a small shape. Use the side of your pencil point to fill in the shape. Rub your finger over the shape and see how far you can smear the pencil around the edges of the shape. Draw

another shape and fill a small section of it with pencil. See if you can smear the pencil to fill in the rest of the shape.

Draw a real or imaginary animal and try smudging the pencil lines to make it look fuzzy, shaded, or shiny.

Nib Magic

A can of pen and ink materials can help the children make pictures, even when the ink blots!

Materials:
- plastic sheet
- small jar of water
- pen holder and nibs
- small bottle of ink
- scrap paper
- brushes
- drinking straws, twigs, sticks
- paper towels or napkins

Directions

Spread the plastic cloth over your desk. Put some water in the small jar. Stick one of the nibs in the pen holder. Dip the nib in the ink. Draw on a piece of scrap paper with the pen. See how long you can draw before you have to dip the pen in the ink again.

Brush water on a piece of scrap paper. Draw on the wet paper with the pen and ink; see what happens to the ink when it touches the wet paper.

Put a drop of ink on a dry piece of paper. With a straw, blow the ink in different directions. When you have blown the ink as far as it will go, look at the design you have made. With your pen and ink, make a picture out of your design.

Dampen a piece of paper with a wet napkin. Use the pen and ink to draw on the wet paper.

Wet a sheet of paper. Use the pen and ink to make a dot drawing on the wet paper.

Wet a sheet of paper. With a brush, make ink blots on the paper. Place another sheet of paper on the first one and press the sheets together. Look at the ink blots on the papers. Draw pen and ink pictures, using the ink blots in your pictures.

A Can of Colored Marking Pens

A rainbow of marking pens is guaranteed to inspire even the most timid artist. Use this can with the monster maker on page 24 or use it in the magic castle.

Materials:
- colored marking pens with thick and extra-fine points
- paper and newspapers

Directions

Make your own coloring book from heavy paper, cut into ten 8″ x 8″ squares. Choose an episode from a favorite book or TV program. Draw the pictures for your coloring book with a black marking pen, drawing an outline around everything you plan to color. Using the black marking pen, draw an outline of the main character. Draw as many of the characters as you want to. Draw a scene showing where most of the action takes place. Draw a picture of the most exciting things that happens in the story. Draw a picture of the conclusion of the adventure. Draw a picture of yourself with some of the characters in the story. Color the pictures with the colored marking pens.

A Can of Fingerprint Magic

Materials:
- stamp pad
- napkin
- jar of ink cleaner
- scrap paper
- fine-point black pens

Directions

Press your little finger down on the stamp pad and then press it on a piece of paper. Make a pattern of little-finger and thumb prints. Make an animal out of thumb and little-finger prints. Make ten different kinds of animals using your fingerprints and a few black pen lines. Make a set of number cards using the ten different creations: on one card make one creature. On the second card put two other creatures. Continue to stamp your finger animals on the cards until you have a tenth card with ten creatures on it.

Use your fingerprints to make a circus scene. Make a clown, a ring master, a dancing bear, a trapeze artist, a juggler, a lion, a seal, and some monkeys. Draw pen lines to finish your picture.

A Can of Scratchboard

Materials:
- white cardboard or commercial scratch-board
- pencil
- crayons
- india ink and brush
- sharp pointed pin or etching tool

Directions

Lightly sketch a pencil design or drawing on the cardboard. Color the drawing with crayon, applying the crayon as heavily as possible. Put several coats of different colors on the drawing. Then paint india ink over the crayon. Brush ink over every spot until the drawing is totally covered. Let it dry completely. With a sharp point—a pin, needle, scissors, or etching tool—scratch away the ink, making a design with the crayon colors.

More Cans of Illustration Techniques

Charcoal

Fill a can with charcoal pencils, sandpaper, gum eraser, paper scraps, napkins, or paper towels.

Linoleum Blocks

Fill a can with rubber stamps, paper and pens, and stamp pads of several colors.

Silhouette

Fill a can with black and white paper, fingernail scissors, and glue.

Cut and Paste

Fill a can with colored paper, glue, and scissors.

The A-B-Z Printery

In this center, children stamp out poems, sentences, cards, posters, bulletin-board headings and labels, charts, monthly and weekly calendars, spelling lists, story starters, tongue twisters, riddles, and rhymes.

Materials:
- commercial or homemade stamp sets
- stamp pads
- letter stencils
- pieces of paper and cardboard

Stamp Sets

Materials:
- typography book and photocopy machine
- Eberhard Faber 6004 green erasers
- plastic triangle
- X-acto knife
- pencil
- stamp pad
- scratch paper

From a typography book, choose a simple alphabet for your first stamp set; letters without serifs are best. Make a photocopy of the set you like and cut out each letter. Rub the side of a pencil point over the wrong side of each letter, filling it in completely. Draw the letters on the eraser backwards so that they will print in the right direction. Then place the penciled-in side of the letter facedown on an eraser. Rub the other side of the letter with a pencil to transfer the pencil impression onto the eraser.

To cut the stamp, place the edge of the small triangle against a straight side of the letter imprint. Insert the X-acto knife at one end, and pressing gently, pull the knife along the triangle's edge. Cut the edge in one stroke; if you remove the blade before the entire edge is cut, the edge will be jagged. If the knife blade is sharp, it will cut through ¼″ with very

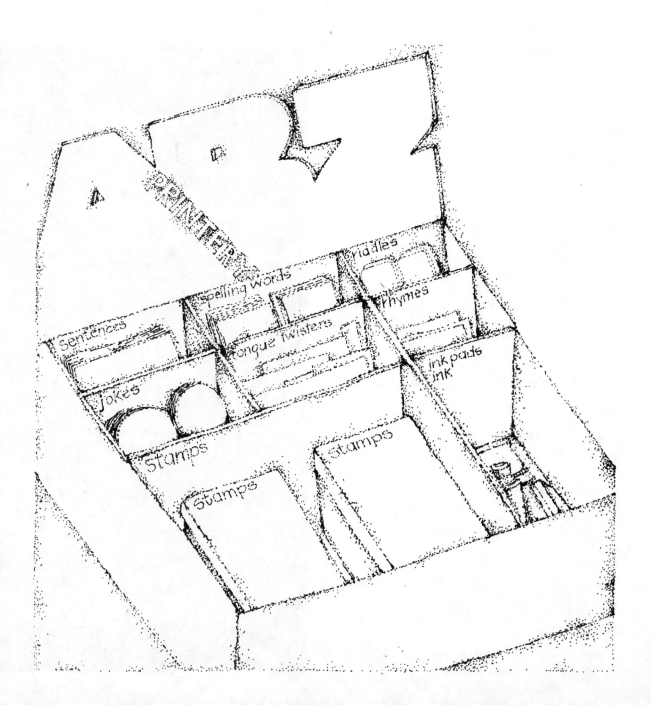

little pressure. More pressure is not necessary and may cause an accident. Use the triangle and knife to cut along each straight edge of the letter. For curved sides, insert the knife at a corner. Instead of turning the knife, turn the eraser as you gently pull the knife around. With your fingernail or with a pair of tweezers pull the sides of each cut edge apart. Insert the X-acto knife and cut the flap of eraser away from the letter. Save eraser scraps and use them to cut out assorted shapes as illustrated. As each letter is completed, gently press it onto a stamp pad and then stamp the letter on scratch paper. If there is a crooked edge, correct it before you do more stamping.

Cutting an alphabet takes time and great care. The first letters will take a long time to cut, but as you cut each letter, you'll learn little tricks and movements, developing confidence and working more quickly. After you've mastered a large simple alphabet, try a smaller, more complicated one.

Foam Letters

Materials:
- art foam
- lightweight cardboard
- letter patterns from a typography book, cardboard patterns, or commercial stencils
- scissors, glue, pencil
- stamp pad with roller-ball dispenser

Art foam is best suited to making large, simple letters 4″ or larger. Cut letter patterns from heavy paper. Turn the patterns over and trace around them onto the foam. Cut them out with scissors. Glue each letter onto a piece of cardboard with tiny dots of glue, being careful that the glue doesn't saturate the foam so that it won't print. Ink the letter with stamp-pad ink that comes with a roller-ball dispenser. Use the stamp sets to make samples for the center.

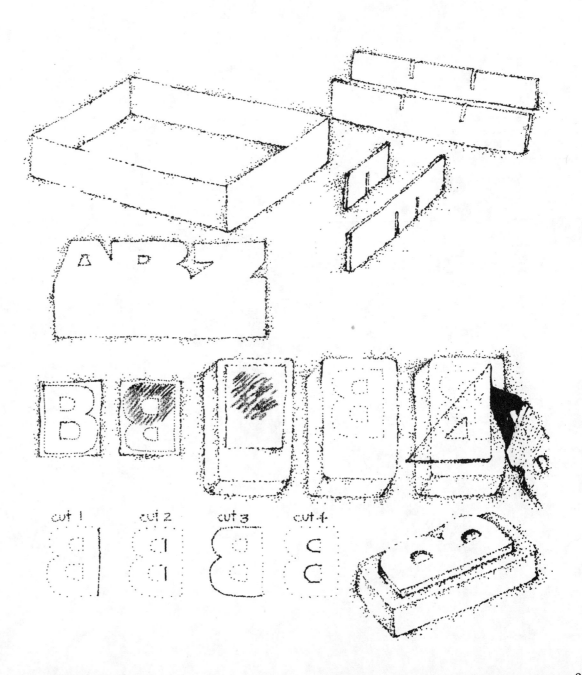

The Secret Garden

In this center, children learn about and make decorative folk art and folk designs from different cultures. The materials required will vary depending on the craft but will always include books or pictures of folk designs. Paper crafts make a good start because most of the crafts can be done with colored tissue paper or construction paper, scissors, glue, and marking pens. You might want to use some of these paper crafts: paper folding (origami, Polish paper cuts, Chinese paper cuts); Christmas cards and valentines; quilling; paper sculpture; torn paper; paper mosaics. This learning center could include activities in which similar crafts from two different cultures are compared.

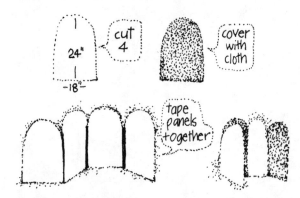

Make this center out of the cardboard panels described in chapter 1, covering them with felt. For each craft, make a sample to illustrate each step. These step-by-step samples can be made by volunteers or by students who have learned the craft at home or elsewhere. Pin the step-by-step samples to the cardboard, writing directions on pieces of paper and pinning them beside each sample as shown. Include a set of variations for children to try after they have mastered the basic craft. The activity shown is an example of a simple craft that could be used in the secret garden.

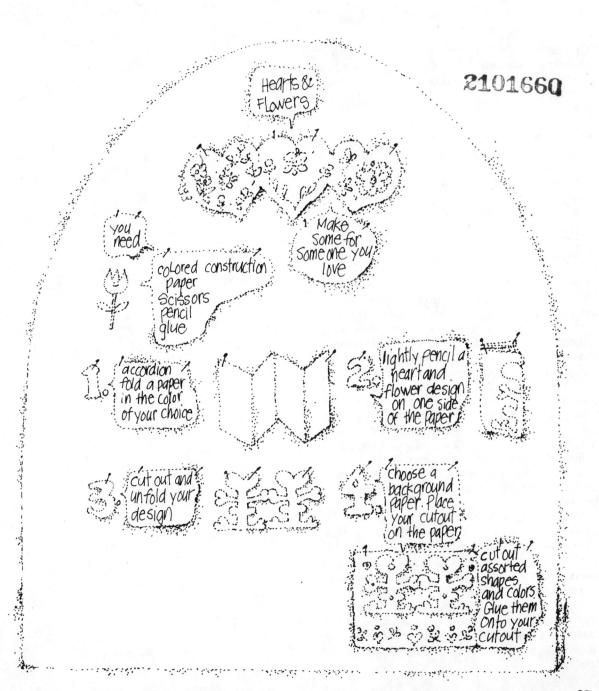

The Surprise Center

This center is for anyone who likes to wrap and unwrap gifts or who loves surprises. It can be a reward center or a rainy-day center.

Materials:
- empty containers
- surprises—a new game, book, puzzle, crossword puzzle, task card for solving a mystery, box of brand-new crayons or pens, pack of cards, anything your students will enjoy
- a box full of wrapping paper
- ribbon
- yarn
- tape

Begin by wrapping five to ten surprises. When children come to the center they choose a package, unwrap it, and play with it. If it is a game for two or more children, they may choose others to play with. After the game is over, the children must rewrap the surprise. They may wrap it any way they wish.

Whenever you add a new game or activity ask for volunteer giftwrappers. There are always children eager to wrap gifts. Encourage the children to make their wrapping a work of art. Some may choose to make the wrapping reflect the contents. Others may enjoy making fancy ribbons and bows. Some may want to make three-dimensional ornaments for the packages.

When used as a reward center, the surprise center might include boxes of tiny surprises. The boxes might hold small toys, books, crayons, or charms or stickers for children to keep. Some boxes could contain coupons redeemable for privileges or gifts later on.

Use this center during the holidays for wrapping gifts the children have made in the classroom. Some children enjoy wrapping their art work to take home to parents or to give to teachers.

SURPRISE
1. Choose a package.
2. Unwrap and use it.
3. Wrap it up with fancy paper and ribbons.

Grab Bag

Materials:
- brown lunch bags
- colored yarn
- index cards for tasks or treats—games, puzzles, question sheets, research questions, codes to decode
- a special bag or box of self-checking materials for the task cards

This center is a variation of the surprise center. Instead of gift-wrapped boxes, the grab bag contains bags tied with yarn. Each bag holds a treat or task card.

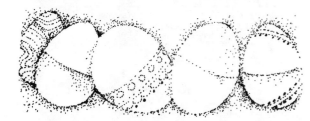

Use an egg carton and twelve colorful plastic eggs to hold the tasks or treats. Use a golden egg for answers.

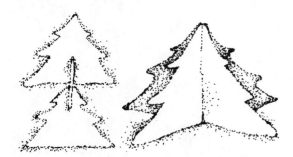

For a special treat put the tasks or treats in brightly colored foil bags. At Christmas the bags might be filled with ingredients for these different holiday crafts: styrofoam balls, sequins and pins, scraps of colored foil, fingernail scissors, glue, gold stars and red tissue paper, yarn scraps in Christmas colors, cranberries and a needle and thread, colored paper strips and tape for paper chains, old-fashioned clothespins, cloth scraps, and yarn and glue to make ornament people.

Use the grab bag to introduce art supplies that you have a limited number of—not enough for the whole class to work with.

The Silly Center

Every classroom has its share of sillies, including the teacher at times. This center structures that silliness into something productive. It helps real sillies learn to control their bursting silliness and to add to instead of detract from the class. After all, too little silliness is as much a problem as too much. Fill this center with riddles, jokes, tongue twisters, and nonsensical or silly activities. Make the center look silly: write everything backwards, upside down, or in silly rebuses. Use mirror writing. Give the center a presiding silly person.

Materials:
- mirror
- makeup crayons

Glue a mirror in the middle of the silly center for reading mirror writing and making silly faces. Include a box of makeup crayons so children can put on silly faces before reciting silly poems or tongue twisters. The makeup can serve as a mask for serious students to hide behind while they have a bit of fun.

Here is a game of silly questions to play in the silly center. Make a stack of cards with the names of well-known sillies from sources your students have access to, such as Sesame Street or books found in the classroom. Each player draws a card. Then each player can ask twenty questions to try to guess the characters on the other players' cards. Some possible sillies are a clown, Miss Piggy, Mork, or Oscar the Grouch.

The following activities are additional things the children can do in the silly center:
- Write, illustrate, and solve riddles.
- Practice tongue twisters.
- Memorize well-known nonsensical verses, such as those written by Edward Lear, Lewis Carroll, or Dr. Seuss. Write or stamp out those verses and illustrate them.
- Make up their own nonsense rhymes using the week's spelling words.

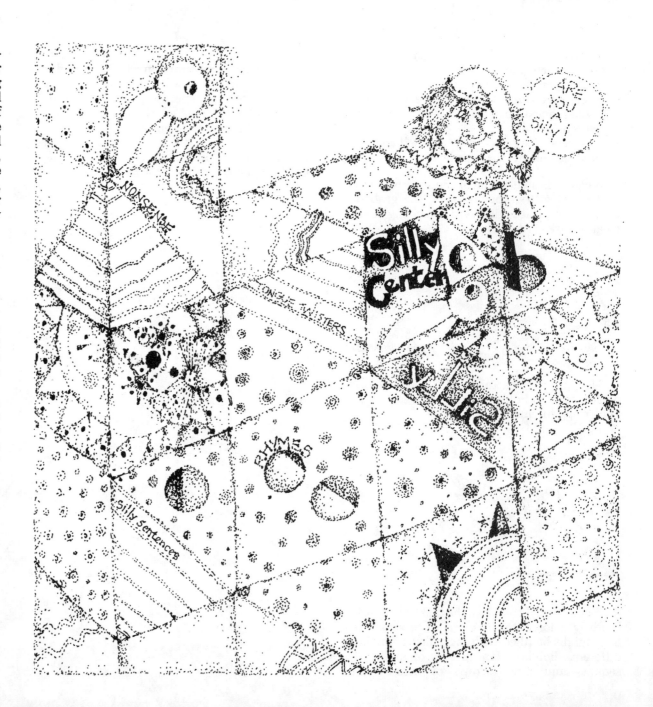

Twenty-Six Flavors

This center features monthly flavor lists available from several well-known ice-cream franchises. Students alphabetize the flavors and make up new flavors to add to the list.

Make twenty-six construction paper ice-cream cones and laminate or cover them with clear contact paper. On each cone, write an ice-cream flavor that begins with a different letter of the alphabet; use a flavor list from an ice-cream store, making up flavors if you need to complete the alphabet. Cut out long strips of paper and put them in the center with the cones.

Send the children to the center and ask them to arrange the cones in alphabetical order. Each child takes one of the long paper strips and draws a picture of each cone on it, writing a flavor underneath each cone in alphabetical order.

Have the children invent their own flavor alphabets, giving the flavors silly or serious names. Help them to make up a list of rhyming flavors, such as nutty-putty and tutti-frutti.

Show the children how to make a book in the shape of an ice-cream cone. Invent recipes for each flavor and put them in the book.

Make up a recipe for a sundae or a banana split, listing the ingredients in alphabetical order.

The Cartoon Strip

In this center, students write and illustrate cartoons individually and as a class.

Materials:
- bulletin board sectioned into cartoon-strip frames or folded cardboard covered with cloth, as illustrated
- construction paper
- plain paper
- pencils and pens
- scissors
- pins
- duplicating master for making blank cartoon strips
- a box or collection of old photos or magazines
- pictures
- old comic books and cartoon strips

If you use a wall bulletin-board, make the cartoon frames 15″ high and anywhere from 15″ to 30″ wide. Divide the board into sections with colored yarn or strips of cloth stapled onto the board.

For a cartoon strip created by the class, have students make characters out of construction paper. They can be made as movable figures (page 50) or as permanent cloth characters with details sewn or glued onto a cloth background. Start the cartoon strip by asking interested students to draw characters for the strip. Have them draw the figures in a variety of positions. Students who like to draw may want to assume responsibility for drawing one character daily. Rotate the task if others are interested. A daily class session could determine the adventures to be illustrated and captioned. Have students use spelling and vocabulary words in the daily or weekly strips.

This activity may start some children on their own cartoons. Provide a place for them to display their cartoons. These cartoon strips

could be drawn onto ditto masters and run off for the class and for other classrooms.

Make up a set of cartoon-starter task cards for children who need some ideas and inspiration.

Make a cartoon-character maker following the directions for the monster maker on page 24, changing the dials to describe cartoon characters rather than monsters.

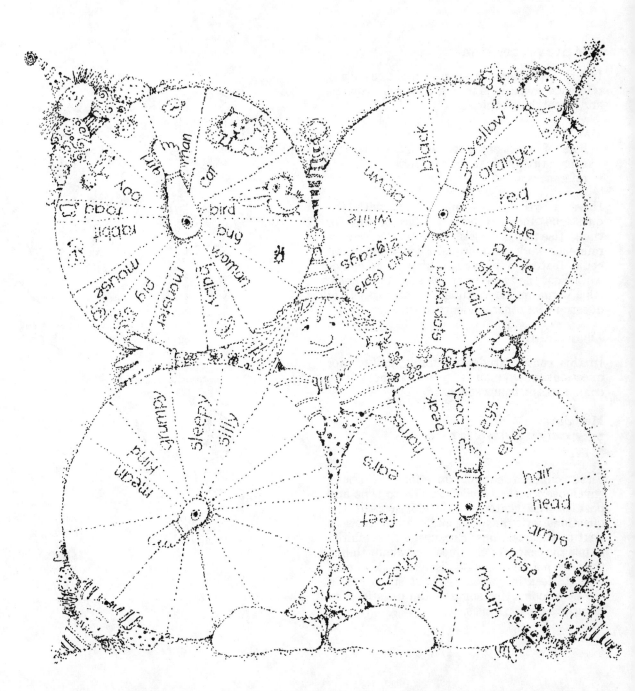

Assorted Learning Centers

The Scavenger Hunt

In this center, students practice using reference sources, planning research projects, and researching topics.

Materials:

- lists of questions obtained from reference sources available to the students
- references

Have a weekly scavenger hunt with ten questions about a person, place, event, or thing. Use true or false statements that require reference work for answers. Each week's hunt could feature a particular kind of reference work. Post the answers at the end of the week. As a variation, have students make up sets of questions for other students to answer.

Dear Gabby

In this center, students submit and answer questions anonymously, just as the advice columnists do in newspapers.

Materials:

- typewriter and typing paper
- paper

First, children submit questions in sealed envelopes for the teacher or aide to type and post in the center. The children read the questions, write answers, and post the answers next to the questions. Encourage the children to use the center to ask questions about things they are not comfortable discussing. You may want to feed in questions about situations in the classroom. Use some of the questions as group-discussion topics.

The Model Center

There seems to be a universal fascination for making tiny versions of everything—cars, boats, planes, houses, trains, and people.

A project for the model center might include a relief map, replicas of the boats Columbus sailed across the sea, an African village, or a miniature landscape of the old west with a model train running through it. Materials will vary with the project you choose.

Soap Opera

Students dial characters and situations to make up their own soap-opera tragedies or comedies. This activity is something that the students add to daily, like the cartoon center.

Materials:
- cardboard
- compass
- spinners
- paper fasteners
- marking pens

Make dials like the ones described for the monster maker on page 24, asking students to contribute ideas. One dial should list characters by name, title, or occupation, for example, Joe, brother, doctor. On a second dial, write soap-opera situations—"lost at sea," "caught in an elevator with x," "unloved by y," "loved by z."

Students spin the dials and then write what their characters do in the particular situation. Then they pin up their story in the center. Their daily task is to weave new events into previous stories. To add variety, make a third dial that names both new characters and new situations.

Use this center as a source for group discussion of serious and humorous situations.

Recipe Box

This center focuses on good nutrition.

Materials:
- magazine pictures of food
- marking pens
- paper or index cards
- chart paper

Decorate a box or triptych with pictures of food, can labels, and other food containers. Feature weekly recipes for children to copy, take home, and cook for themselves. Invite children to bring in their favorite recipes and to post them for other students to copy and try out. Change the focus each month. Feature nutritious snacks one month. During the first week, post recipes to copy. In the second week, have students think of and test new snack ideas. In the third week, feature snacks from other cultures. During the fourth week, have students bring in recipes that are traditions in their families—snacks for celebrations or for any special time.

Dear Diary

In this center, students improve their writing skills, learning to keep diaries and inventing possible entries for famous people.

Materials:
- paper and pencils
- diaries of famous people

Show the students how to make and keep small diaries following the directions on page 90. Put daily questions in the center to encourage the students to write about a variety of things.

Include excerpts from famous diaries. Rather than writing their own diaries, students could invent entries famous people might make in their diaries.

Folk Tales

This center could be a listening post or a collection of books. Use this center to introduce folk tales, to compare tales from different cultures, and to inspire the writing of modern folk tales. Ask students to read three similar stories, to find the common element in the stories, and then to write a contemporary version or a version appropriate to a culture being studied.

What's It For?

Students guess the functions of assorted unusual objects.

Materials:
- unusual objects (gadgets, antiques, oddities)
- index cards
- pencils
- cards that describe actual use of each object

Display one of the objects in the center. On the index cards, students write what they think the object is used for, where it came from, what it is made of, and any other speculations they want to make about it.

The cards are posted in the center. A card that describes the actual use of the object is posted among the students' cards. Then students vote on the card that they think gives the best explanation. Whoever submits or chooses the correct description is asked to submit the next unusual object. Sometimes a picture or drawing of an object can be used in place of the actual object itself.

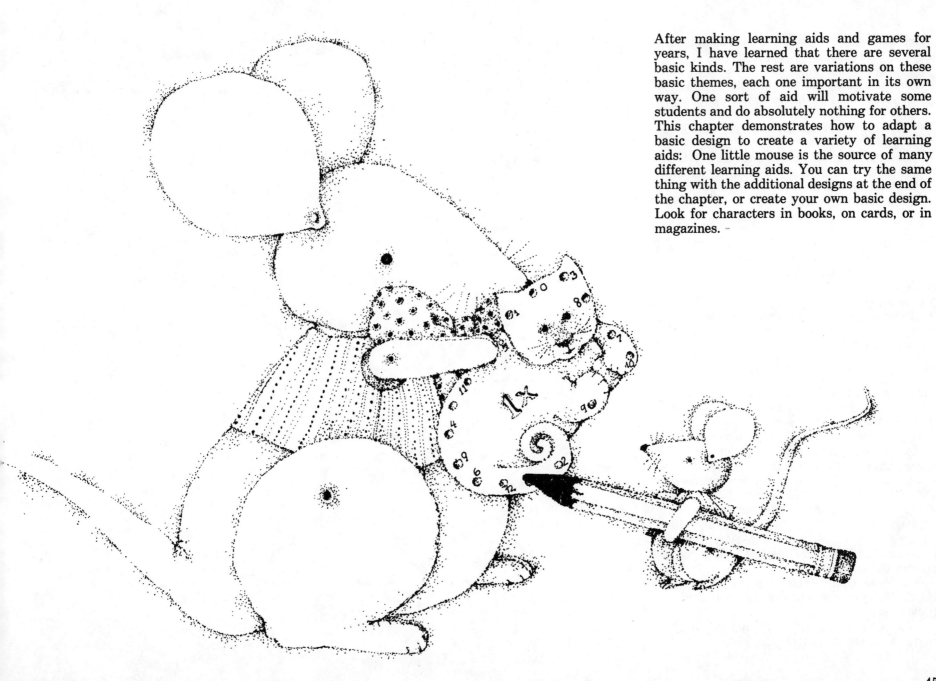

After making learning aids and games for years, I have learned that there are several basic kinds. The rest are variations on these basic themes, each one important in its own way. One sort of aid will motivate some students and do absolutely nothing for others. This chapter demonstrates how to adapt a basic design to create a variety of learning aids: One little mouse is the source of many different learning aids. You can try the same thing with the additional designs at the end of the chapter, or create your own basic design. Look for characters in books, on cards, or in magazines.

Enlarging a Basic Design

Here are some methods for enlarging your basic mouse design.

- Shoot a slide of the mouse design and project it onto a white sheet of paper taped on the wall.
- Project the original design with an opaque projector.
- Trace the original design onto an overhead-projector transparency, tape a paper onto the wall behind the projector, and draw the design on the paper.

Materials:
- transparent enlargement grids
- fine-point black marking pen
- tape
- tracing paper
- tissue paper and marking pens or carbon paper
- paper or cloth

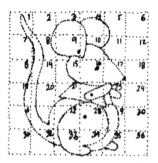

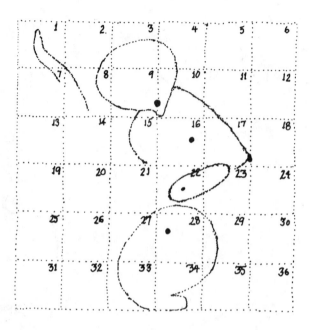

Make or purchase a set of transparent enlargement grids in an assortment of sizes. You can make your own grid paper on transparent paper or acetate. With a ruler, mark half-inch intervals along each side of a piece of paper. Draw lines from side to side and from top to bottom. Make another grid that has ¾" squares, and other grids with 1", 1½", 2", 2½", and 3" squares. If you cannot buy transparent grid paper with 1/8" and 1/3" squares, make those also. These transparent grids can be placed over designs to help you to enlarge the designs more accurately by hand if you are not comfortable drawing them free-hand. Number the squares on each grid as illustrated.

To begin enlarging your mouse design, place a small grid over the picture of the

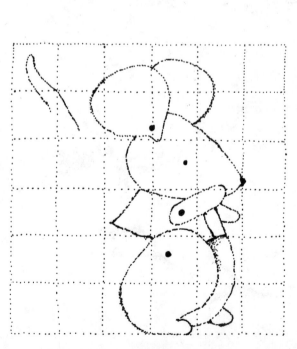

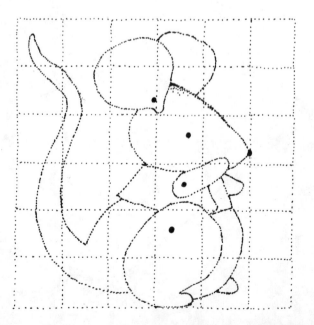

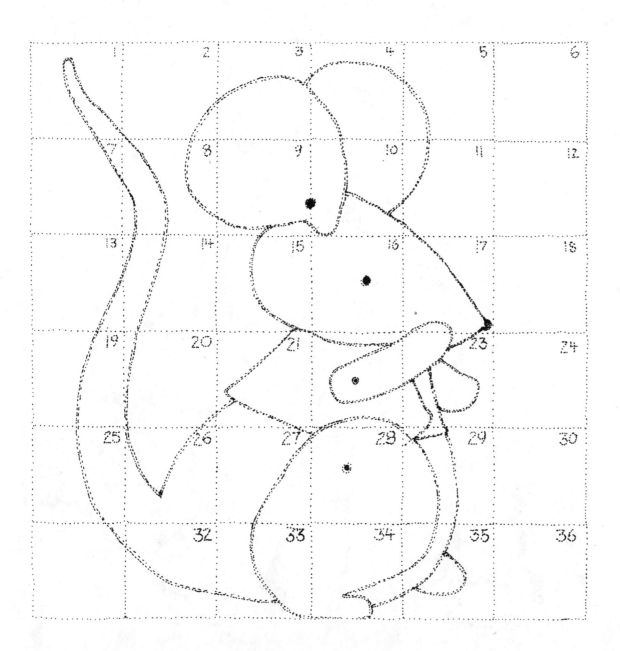

mouse, taping the grid so that it won't slip. Place a larger grid under a piece of tracing paper. To double the size of the mouse, select a grid that has squares twice as big as the squares on the grid taped over the mouse. If you have a 1/4″ grid over a 2″ high mouse and you want to make a mouse 8″ high, then you need to place a grid with 1″ squares under the tracing paper. That way the finished mouse will be four times its original height or 8″. If you want to make a 16″ mouse, then place a grid with 2″ squares under the tracing paper.

Once you have chosen the proper grids, tape them in place and locate the number of the square at the upper left-hand corner of the design. Find the square with that number on your large grid; with a light pencil line, draw in the square whatever you see in the corresponding square of the smaller grid. Then use the same method to fill in the next square. Continue to duplicate what you see in each square. When you finish, look at the whole drawing and correct anything that looks funny. Add details. Go over pencil lines with a fine-point black marking pen. If you are going to use the drawing as a pattern, cut it out or place it under another sheet of tracing paper and make another copy.

To reduce a large design, reverse this process, placing a large grid over the design and copying it onto a smaller grid. To use your pattern, make a pencil tracing of it on white tissue paper. Tape the tissue over the paper or cloth you want to make the design on. Go over the pencil lines with a marking pen that will bleed slightly—just enough to make repeated small dots on the paper or cloth underneath. Then connect the dots and cut out the design.

Now that you know how to draw a mouse in any size, you can use one small mouse to make a number of aids. If you want a house for your mouse, look on page 75.

Fingertip Mice

For a mouse that will sit on your finger, cut out a ½″ x 1½″ strip of paper. Glue the strip into a ring to fit your finger, and glue a small cutout of the mouse onto the ring. Make ten mouse rings and put them on your fingers. Hold up your hands and have the children count all the tiny mice.

Instead of making a paper ring, make two paper mice in the same size but facing in opposite directions. Tape or glue them back to back along the outside edges. Do not glue the tops or bottoms together. Slip your finger in between the two mice. Now you have a mouse no matter which way your hand turns.

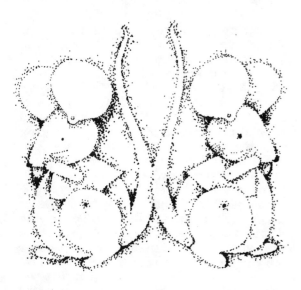

Make another collection of fingertip mice by gluing ten mouse heads onto ten peanut shells. Cut out ten pairs of ears and eyes, ten noses, and ten sets of whiskers; glue the mouse faces on ten peanut shells.

48

Flannelboard Mouse

Use this mouse as a flannelboard character. Make the flannelboard mouse out of construction paper, lightweight cardboard, or cloth. If you make it out of paper or cardboard, glue pieces of flannel or sandpaper to the back so it will stick to the flannelboard.

For a flannelboard mouse with movable arms and legs, cut out separate arms and legs and attach them to the body with paper fasteners. Glue sandpaper on the back of the head and body and on each arm and leg. Make outfits with tabs, like paper-doll clothes, to use as costumes. Make two mice to tell "The Tale of Two Bad Mice" and three mice for "Three Blind Mice."

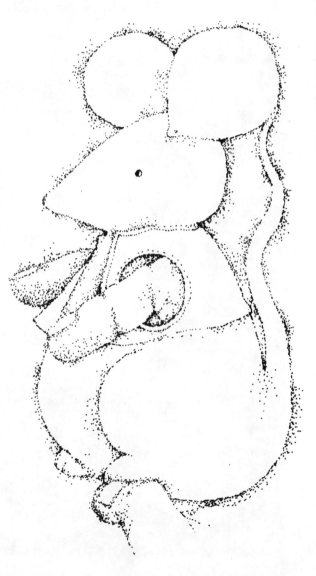

To make a tiny stuffed mouse, place a pattern of the mouse design on a double thickness of felt. Cut out the mouse, making separate arms, legs, and ears. Use a blanket stitch to sew the double thicknesses together. Stuff the arms, legs, and body with cotton or polyester stuffing. Attach the arms, legs, and ears to each side of the mouse, taking stitches that go from one side all the way through the mouse's body to the opposite side.

If you want to use the small stuffed mouse as a finger puppet, leave it open at the bottom so that you can stick your finger in it. Embroider eyes and a nose on the mouse. For whiskers, stiffen thread with glue; glue dried thread onto the mouse's face. Dress your mouse in a few felt scraps, adding a bit of ribbon or lace and one or two buttons. You may want to dress your mouse in a costume.

Make a large mouse with arms that are as big as your fingers. Place a piece of tracing paper over the enlarged mouse. Draw everything on the mouse but its arms. Instead of drawing arms, draw two holes, each one large enough for a finger to fit through. Cut out the mouse, making sure to cut out the two holes. Use this pattern to make a mouse out of heavy paper. Color the mouse with crayons or marking pens. Put your fingers through the holes and you'll have a finger puppet with movable arms.

Shadow Puppets

Materials:
- lightweight cardboard or black construction paper
- scissors
- paper fasteners
- thread
- nylon thread or thin florist's wire
- overhead projector

An overhead-projector stage is 8″ x 10″. Make a mouse one-third to one-half that size or in a size that is proportionate to the other characters in the story. Cut each part of the mouse—head, body, arms, and legs—out of black paper. Using a loose stitch, sew the arms and legs onto the body. They should be loose enough to allow free movement. Sew a 10″ piece of nylon thread on each hand and foot; the threads are used to manipulate the puppet. Glue short pieces of thread on the face for whiskers. Put the mouse on the projector stage and try to move it. You may prefer to attach the arms and legs to thin pieces of florist's wire—the stiffness of the wire makes it easier to control the puppet. Props and other characters for the puppet play can be made, like silhouettes, out of black construction paper.

Glue fake fur onto cardboard cutouts

Mouse Cards

Materials:
- lightweight cardboard
- mouse stamp
- stamp pad

Use the basic mouse design on a set of game cards. Make a mouse stamp following the directions on page 32 or make a larger stamp out of art foam (page 33). To make a deck of cards with four different suits, stamp one mouse shape in four different colors or cut four different mouse shapes and stamp them on the cards as shown. Stamp numbers or letters on the cards. Use the mouse stamp to make a set of classification cards. Make stamps in many different kinds of mouse shapes, or vary the cards by stamping the mouse in different positions. Cut large cards and then stamp configurations of several mice on them.

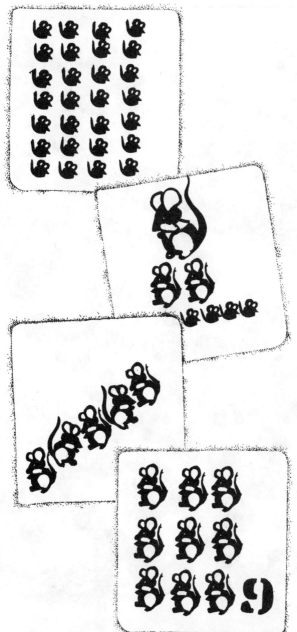

Mouse Math

Materials:
- mouse stamp
- stamp pad
- cardboard bottle caps or small pieces of cardboard

Make a very small mouse stamp about ½″ long and stamp the mouse on a number of cardboard bottle caps. Instead of counting beans or fingers, show the children how to count mice stamped on cardboard bottle caps or on small pieces of lightweight cardboard. Have the students use the mouse stamp and a stamp pad to represent equations on scrap paper. To see that students don't get tired of mice, make a variety of small stamps for children to use for math practice.

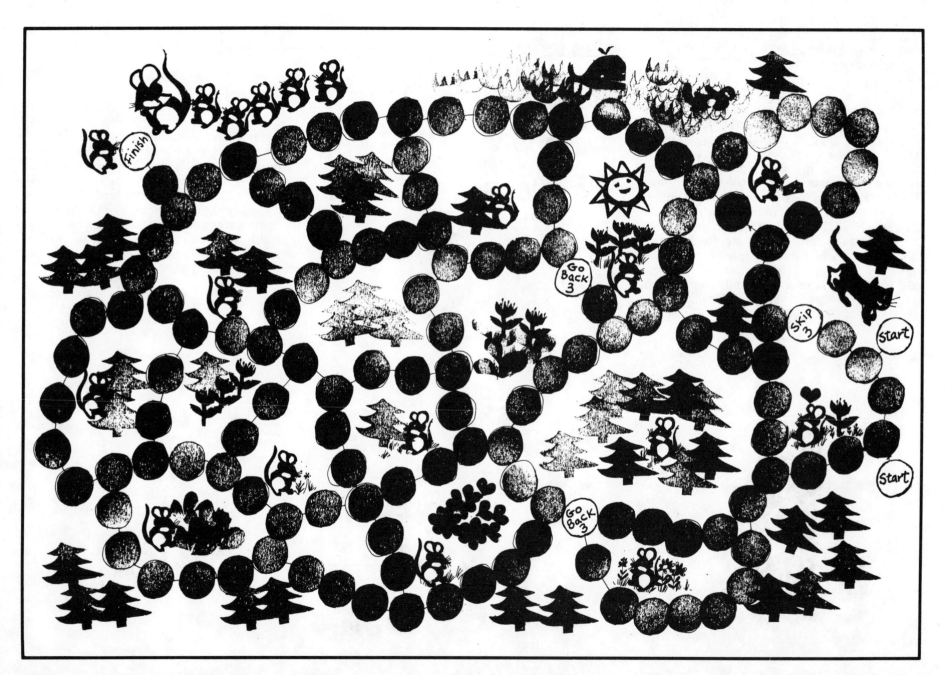

Cat and Mouse Gameboard

Materials:
- art foam or eraser stamps
- stamp pad
- lightweight cardboard
- magazine cutouts or torn paper
- dice or cardboard spinner

Make a cat stamp following the directions on page 32. On a lightweight piece of cardboard, draw a path marked off in 1″ spaces. Stamp the mouse along the road. Then use other stamp shapes to create a landscape surrounding the road. The illustration will give you an idea of what to do with a few stamps. Make scenery out of magazine cutouts or torn paper. Stamp the cat onto lightweight cardboard several times and cut out the cats to use as markers. Players take turns rolling the dice or spinning the spinner to determine who moves and how far.

Stand-Up Mouse

Make a stand-up cardboard mouse of almost any size by cutting a strip of cardboard as long as the mouse is high and half as wide as the mouse. Use masking tape or cloth mystic-tape to attach the strip to the middle of the mouse's back lengthwise, as shown. Tape the strip on both sides so that the tape forms a hinge.

Mouse Paperdolls

Make a mouse paperdoll in any size. For a bulletin board, make a mouse 2″ high out of butcher paper or pieces of a cardboard box. Make an assortment of clothes for the mouse to wear depending on the weather, season, or holiday. To make clothes for the mouse, place the cardboard mouse on a piece of newspaper and trace around it. Cut out the newspaper pattern in sections—the head, upper body, and lower body. Place the upper body on a piece of construction paper and draw a jacket around the tracing as shown, or place the upper and lower bodies together on the sheet of paper to make a dress.

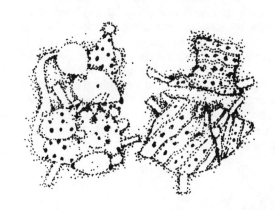

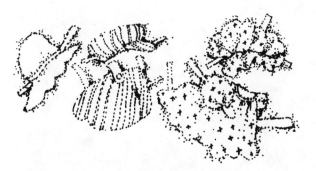

Mouse Pencil-Poke

Draw a mouse that is 12″ high and transfer it to a piece of lightweight cardboard, adding details with a marking pen. Then cut it out. Write a math fact every one to three inches around the edges; for example, 5 x 5, 5 x 6, 5 x 10. Don't write the facts consecutively. After you've written the math facts, punch a hole beside each fact. Then turn the mouse over and write the answers next to the holes.

Two children can use this mouse pencil-poke. One child holds the mouse and pokes a pencil through one of the holes. The other child reads the math fact aloud and guesses the answer. The first child looks for the pencil point on the back to check the answer. Instead of making one pencil poke for each set of math facts, make a few and laminate them. Write the facts in grease pencil or water-soluble pen so that they can be wiped off. Show the children how to make their own pencil pokes. Once the surface is laminated, the children can write out whichever set of facts they are working on. When finished with the set, the children can wipe it off and write a new set on their pencil pokes.

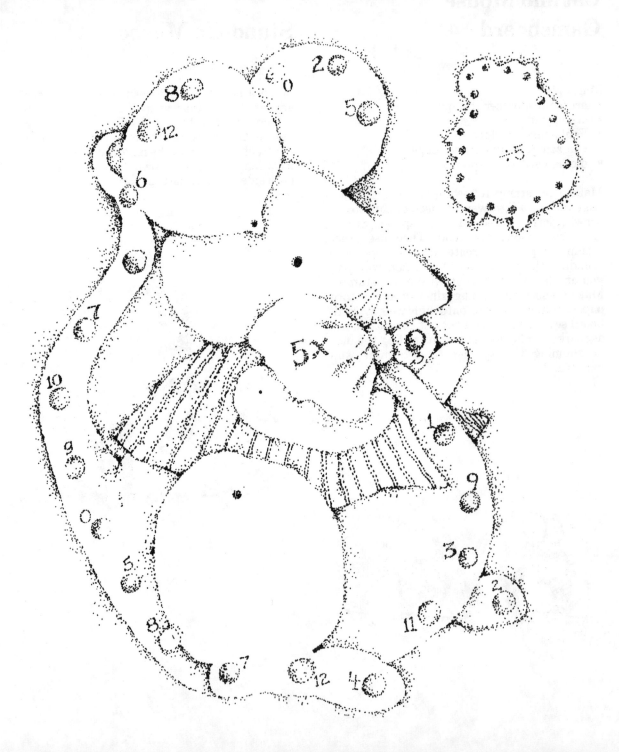

Mouse Mask

Make mouse masks for use in dramatic plays or in musical performances. Enlarge the head of the mouse to 12″ across or large enough to cover a child's face. Transfer the enlargement onto a piece of lightweight cardboard and cut it out. Hold it up to a child's face and use a pencil to mark two spots for the eyes. Then cut holes just large enough for the child to see out of. Color the front of the mask with paints, crayons, or colored paper.

Variations

Enlarge the mouse design to 3-4′ high; make the pattern on several sheets of newspaper taped together. Then transfer the pattern to heavy paper. An opaque projector could save time in making this enlargement. Cut the mouse out. Hold it up to a child's face to figure out where to put the eye holes. You can also cut out a circle in the size of a child's face so that the entire child's face will show through. Paint or collage the mouse. For a mouse this size, you could glue fabric onto the paper; cut away the backs of some old clothes and glue the fronts onto the mouse body. For a special mouse, glue some fake fur or some fuzzy material onto the body.

Monster Mouse

Materials:
- newspapers
- thick-point marking pens and pencil
- white tissue paper or tracing paper
- cardboard boxes
- heavy-duty scissors
- masking tape

Tape newspapers together to form a 6-8' by 8-10' sheet of paper. Draw a large mouse on the paper using a thick-point marking pen. If you have trouble drawing it freehand, make a grid on the newspaper and follow the instructions on page 46 for enlarging designs.

After you've drawn the mouse, divide the drawing into jigsaw-puzzle sections, numbering each section. Place tissue paper or tracing paper over a puzzle piece. Then trace the section and write the number on the tracing. Cut out the tracing and place it on the newspaper drawing. Place each tracing over its original section to check the pieces and to see that you have traced them all. Trace and cut out each puzzle piece.

Cut cardboard boxes into sections. Place the traced jigsaw sections on the cardboard. Trace around them and then cut out the cardboard. Lightly pencil the piece number on the back of the cardboard and place the cardboard sections on the newspaper pattern as you cut them out. Sand away rough-cut edges with a medium-grade sandpaper.

Mix paint to cover the puzzle—be sure to mix enough paint to cover the very large areas. For a longer lasting puzzle, paint with enamel. Paint all the puzzle parts and erase the pencil numbers on the back. Scramble all the parts. Have the children put the puzzle back together.

Variations

Make a giant puzzle in the shape of a dinosaur, boat, bus, rainbow, elephant, or whale.

Mouse Games

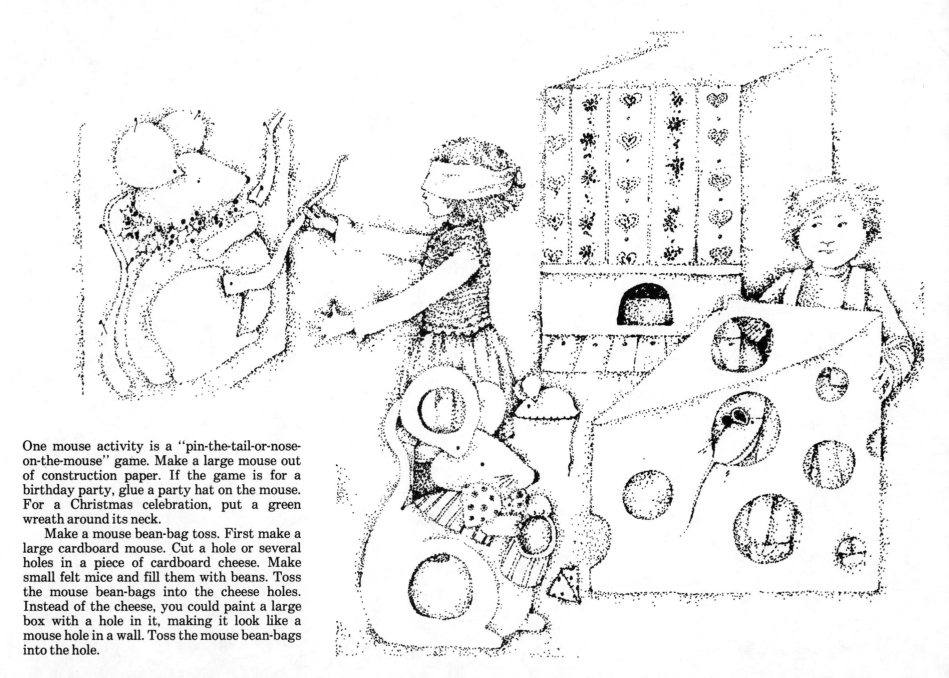

One mouse activity is a "pin-the-tail-or-nose-on-the-mouse" game. Make a large mouse out of construction paper. If the game is for a birthday party, glue a party hat on the mouse. For a Christmas celebration, put a green wreath around its neck.

Make a mouse bean-bag toss. First make a large cardboard mouse. Cut a hole or several holes in a piece of cardboard cheese. Make small felt mice and fill them with beans. Toss the mouse bean-bags into the cheese holes. Instead of the cheese, you could paint a large box with a hole in it, making it look like a mouse hole in a wall. Toss the mouse bean-bags into the hole.

If you don't like the mouse design used in this chapter, perhaps you will find a pattern you like better on one of these pages. These designs can be used for all of the suggested aids and games.

CHAPTER FOUR
PUPPETS

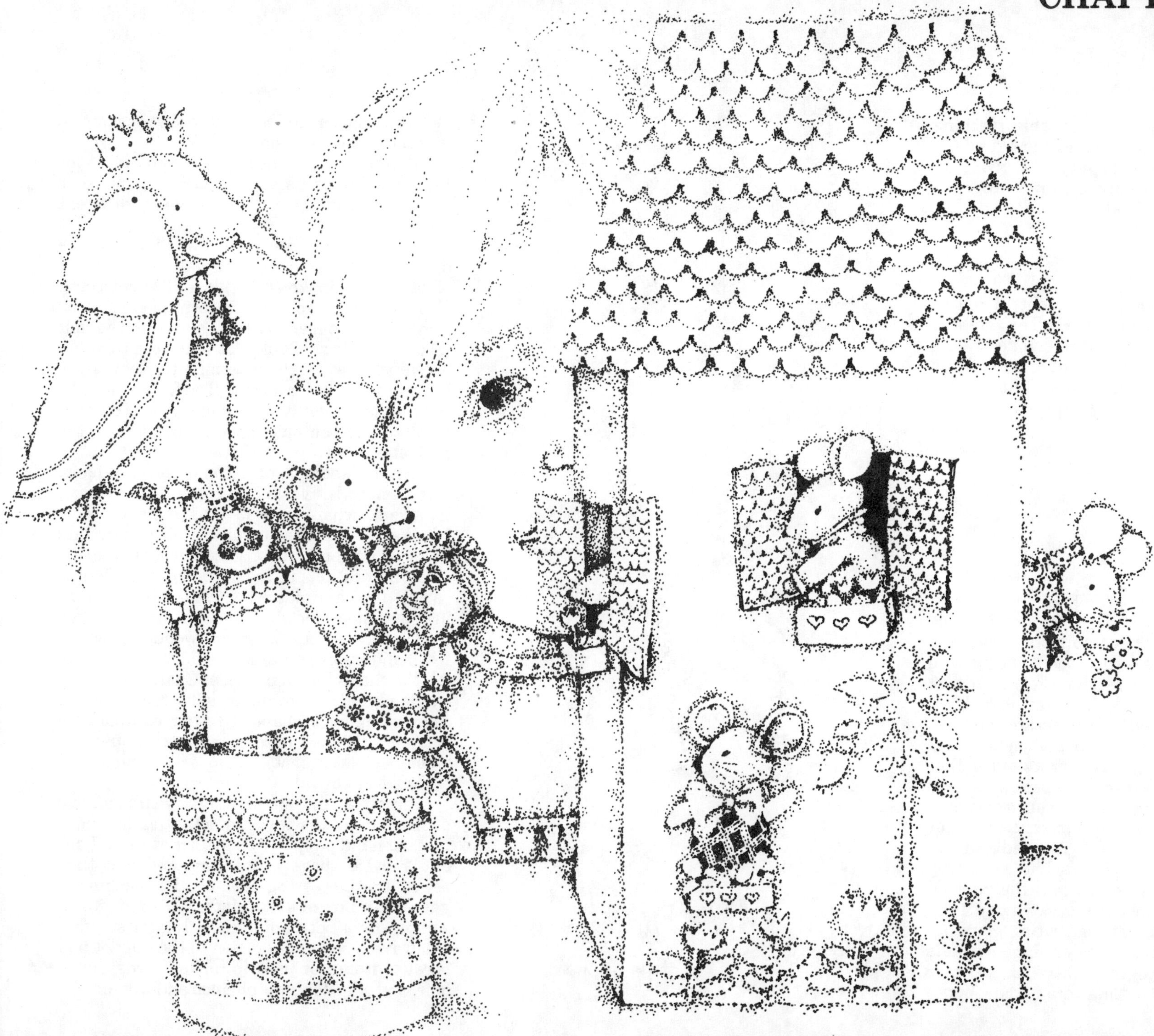

Puppets

Puppets enhance every imaginable teaching situation. No one ever becomes too old or too sophisticated to enjoy a puppet show. Puppetry is magic to young children—an easy magic for them to duplicate.

Felt Hand-Puppets

You can make a hand puppet out of felt in thirty minutes or in ten hours. The ten-hour puppet will be a highly detailed and decorative work of art, but the thirty-minute puppet can be just as creative and just as much fun to play with.

Materials:
- scratch paper and pencil
- felt scraps
- embroidery thread
- needles, pins
- threads
- scissors
- lace, ribbon, buttons, sequins

Felt is a good fabric for puppets because it doesn't fray, it lasts well without facing, and it's easy for children to sew. Felt comes in every color. If you anticipate using a large quantity, contact a felt manufacturer and ask about special offers on bags of bolt ends.

To make a basic pattern for a puppet that will fit your hand or a child's hand, you will need a pencil and paper. Place your hand on a piece of paper with your thumb extended out from your index finger. Your middle finger should extend to the right while your ring finger and pinkie are folded into the palm of your hand. Draw an outline ½″ away from your hand, beginning at your wrist, going up and around your thumb, index finger, middle finger, and down to the other side of your wrist. Around the outline, draw the puppet

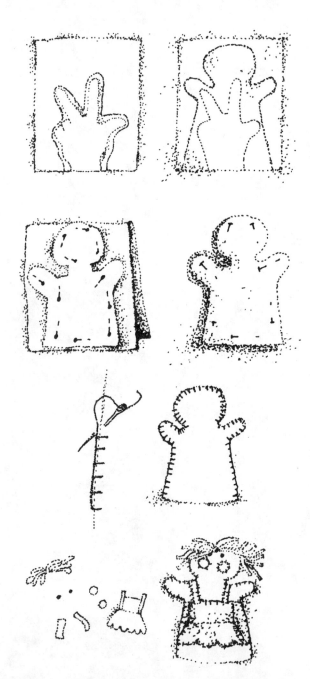

pattern. The outline will insure that the puppet fits the puppeteer's hand.

Illustrations on the next page give ideas for basic hand-puppets. As you can see, one basic pattern can be used to make many different puppets.

Cut out the paper pattern and pin it onto a double thickness of felt. If you want a reversible puppet, make each side a different color. Cut out the two felt pattern pieces. Then remove the paper pattern and pin the felt pieces together. Blanket stitch them together as illustrated, remembering to leave the bottom opening for a hand. The felt can also be sewn together on a sewing machine. You may want to have an aide or volunteer sew up the puppets.

Cut out scraps of colored felt for facial features, tails, vests, dresses, ties, jackets, hats, and whatever else your puppet needs. Blanket stitch these details in place. Use bits of lace, ribbon, buttons, sequins, and other small decorations to finish the puppet. Details can also be embroidered onto the felt. A parent in the school district where I once worked made the most amazing and wonderful set of felt hand-puppets based on *Charlotte's Web*. All the characters and each of Charlotte's webs was embroidered in silver silk thread onto a rounded puppet shape. Of course, Charlotte was also stitched onto each of her webs. The whole set was made from felt scraps and embroidery thread.

Since the time she was three years old, one of my daughter's favorite activities has been making hand puppets. To get her started, I cut out a basic shape to fit her hand and then sewed the pieces together on the machine. I gave her a box of yarn, cloth, lace, and ribbon scraps and a bottle of glue. Polyester stuffing is always a popular addition to the puppet box because it can be used to make beards, fluffy hair, and wigs for little old men and women.

2

2
slit

2
2

cut 2

cut
2

cut
2

cut
1
front

cut
1
back

cut
2

cut
1

cut 2

cut 1

front

cut 1

back

cut 2

cut 2

cut
2

coat

Felt Finger-Puppets

These are miniature versions of the felt hand-puppets on pages 64-65. You may want to use them together with larger puppets since they are especially suitable for portraying small animals, bugs, elves and fairies, or dolls. The patterns on pages 58-61 can be used for finger puppets, too. The nicest thing about finger puppets is that the whole cast of characters fits in and on your hand.

    Here are some basic shapes. Use these to make finger puppets. Cut two pieces of fabric and stitch them together as shown. Use scraps of felt, lace, and ribbon to decorate these little puppets.

Stocking Face-Puppets

Materials:
- old nylon stockings
- polyester stuffing or cotton batting
- needle and pins
- thread
- scissors
- beads
- cloth scraps
- paper and pencil

Cut a piece of stocking 5″ long. Tie a knot in one end of the 5″ tube and stuff the tube with polyester stuffing until it is the size and shape you want. Tie the open end of the stuffed stocking. Stitch through both tied ends to reinforce them. Make facial features by inserting a knotted thread through the spot in which you want to place an eye. From that spot, push the needle out the spot where the other eye will be, gently pulling the thread so that an indentation is made in the first eye. Sew back and forth, pulling the thread each time to make the indentations more distinct. Sew a bead into each eye space. Using flesh-colored thread, take a tuck in the stocking to make a small eyelid over each bead. Practice making assorted eyelids, noses, and lips.

At a craft shop look for beads that will make good eyes and teeth. Put a slight touch of rouge on the cheeks. To make hair, cut yarn into pieces of one length and tie the pieces into small bundles. Sew the bundles onto the puppet's head, beginning at the forehead and continuing until you reach the nape of the neck.

Make a hand-puppet body following the directions for felt hand-puppets on page 64. Decorate the puppet body and head with ribbon, lace, rickrack, beads, buttons, or whatever suits the character of the puppet. Sew the stocking face to the puppet body.

Cloth-Bag Puppets

Materials:
- cloth scraps (felt, flannel, old sheets, velour)
- scissors
- needle
- pins
- thread
- decorative trims

Cut a 12″ x 12″ piece of cloth. Fold it in half, right sides together, making a 6″ x 12″ rectangle. Stitch it together along the 12″ side and one of the 6″ sides. The other side is left open for your hand. Stick your hand inside and push it around so the 12″ seam is in the center of your hand. Push the 6″ seam into two points as shown. Cut off one of the points about 2″ from the top and stitch the cut end shut. That seam is now the back of the puppet's head. The other point is the puppet's nose. Turn the rectangle inside out. Use scraps and trims to make eyes, ears, nose, and whiskers.

This is an easy puppet to make in large quantities for young children. One large bedsheet makes thirty to forty puppets.

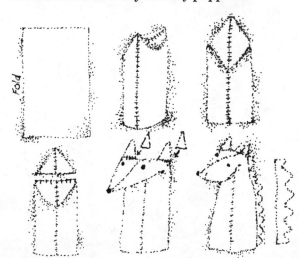

Stuffed-Paper Stick Puppets

Materials:

- newspapers
- paper towel or crepe paper
- cardboard rolls from waxed paper or toilet paper (one roll per puppet)
- colored tissue paper
- masking tape
- yarn, colored ribbon, stickers, feathers
- glue
- scissors

Making these puppets can be a festive activity for a class, a birthday-party crowd, or a child sick in bed.

Wad two sheets of newspaper into a tight ball. Wrap a piece of paper towel around the ball and tie and tape it onto the end of a cardboard roll. Tie a large piece of colored tissue over the ball. Tie it around the neck with a piece of colored ribbon or yarn.

Hair can be made from strips of tissue paper, or yarn can be glued onto the top of the head. Make hats from two pieces of tissue paper cut and glued together as shown. Tell children that only small dabs of glue are needed to hold the paper decorations on the tissue paper.

For a party, you may want to cut decorations in a variety of shapes and sizes and place the cutouts in a box. Fill another box with pre-cut strips for hair. Another box can hold ribbon scraps, bows, feathers, stickers, and any other bright trims that fit the party theme. Children can put a puppet together with these materials in five to ten minutes. Let the puppets dry for thirty minutes.

Variations

Stick puppets come in every size. Make a toothpick version for a dollhouse puppet. Make an 8' giant out of a broomstick—a giant puppet might be an addition to a regular play, especially for monsters or scary characters who hover over the crowd.

To make a large puppet, stuff a large shopping bag with newspapers. Tie a piece of cloth over the bag and tie the bag onto a broomstick or large dowel. Attach a shirt or dress onto the stick and stuff the arms with newspapers. Tie one sleeve onto another stick so that you can make the arm wave. Instead of tying a piece of clothing onto the puppet, tie a large piece of fabric or an old sheet on it.

For elaborate giant puppets, look for old wigs and clothes at a thrift shop. For a lively addition to Halloween festivities, make a scarecrow puppet.

These are only a few of the puppets children can make, but they are good initial projects. The library is filled with books on other kinds of puppets.

71

Puppet Stage

A puppet stage is not essential when you use puppets, but it adds to the fun. Since a stage can be made in a few minutes out of a box or blanket, there is no reason not to have one in the classroom. Children will enjoy making the stage as well as playing with it. Cardboard boxes enable everyone to have a stage, whether it is a tiny finger-puppet box or a larger stage for hand puppets. For children, making the stage is an important part of the puppetry activities. One large puppet theater made out of an appliance box can be used for performances in front of the entire class. The large stage requires an appliance or furniture box. Sometimes you may be able to find an overseas shipping crate. Call a local freight service and ask if they will donate one of their custom freight boxes. These boxes also make fine playhouses.

Materials:
- scratch paper
- pencils
- large cardboard appliance box
- X-acto knife or sharp kitchen knife
- pointed object or tool for scoring cardboard
- sandpaper
- paint (tempera, enamel, acrylic)
- large and small brushes
- paper or cloth for scenery
- crayons
- drop cloth or newspaper
- dowels or curtain rods and beads
- glue

Draw the stage on scratch paper. Sketch the shape of the opening and the decorative designs and colors you wish to use.

With pencil, sketch the stage opening on the box. On the back of the box, sketch a door or an opening for hands. To make a door, sketch it on the box and then cut it open along the top and bottom edges and along one side.

Along the uncut side, make a crease with a sharp pointed object or tool. This crease scores the cardboard making it easier to bend in the exact line desired. Gently bend the cardboard out. This process can be used to make little pop-out holes or doors around the stage. When you cut the front stage opening, instead of removing the cardboard, you may want to cut it down the middle and leave the two sections on the box as doors. Puppets can open the doors just before the play begins. Cut a hole near the front opening for a puppet to make a surprise appearance. Make several holes if you want to have more than one puppet appear outside the stage.

After you've cut all the necessary openings in the box, smooth rough or sharp edges with sandpaper. Poke a hole in each side of the box to hold a dowel or curtain rod. You may want to use several dowels or curtain rods to hang stage curtains and backdrops on which scenes are painted. Ropes can also be strung through the holes and scenery can be hung from the ropes with clothespins. Paint scenery on paper or cloth. The scenery should be on a piece of cloth or paper as wide as the box and about 10″ longer than the stage opening—it needs to be hung 7-10″ above the stage opening so that the rod won't be visible to the audience.

After all doors and holes have been made and sanded, put the box on a drop cloth or newspaper and paint a base coat on it using a background color. If your box is covered with printing, you'll need two coats of paint. When the base coat is dry, lightly pencil the decorations on the box and then paint them. If you draw lightly, the paint will cover your lines. If you use enamel, let the paint dry before painting adjacent areas. Tempera and acrylic paints dry quickly, but they also should be dry before overlapping or immediately adjacent areas are painted. Paint the dowels or curtain rods to match the box. Paint wood

beads to glue at the end of each rod or dowel; the beads will prevent the rods from slipping out of the holes. If you don't want to paint the stage both inside and outside, you can cover it with contact paper or cloth, following the directions on pages 5 and 7.

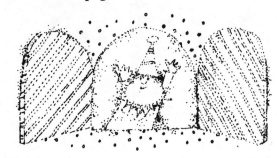

Stage Curtains

Materials:
- cloth
- scissors
- thread
- needles
- pins
- trims (lace, yarn, baubles, gold braid)
- gold or silver textile paint (optional)

For a gathered curtain, you need a piece of fabric twice as wide as the stage opening. Make the curtain 10″ higher than the stage. Cut the fabric into two pieces as shown. Hem the sides and the bottom edge. Turn the top edge over ¼″ and stitch it. Then turn the top edge over 1¼″ or enough for the dowel or curtain rod to slip through. Stitch the edge down. Decorate the curtain with yarn, braid, buttons, or lace, or leave it plain. You may also paint the cloth with textile paint or acrylics. Slide the rod through the two curtains. Slip one end of the rod through the hole and put a wood bead on that end. Insert the other end in the opposite hole and attach a bead to it.

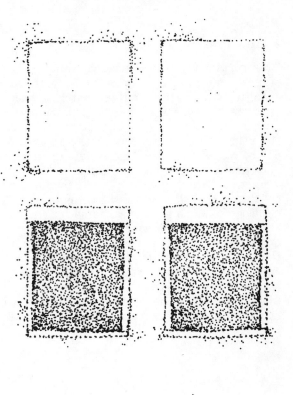

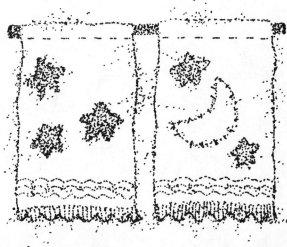

Flap Curtain

This curtain is made the same width as the stage opening and 10″ higher. Sew a yarn loop onto the bottom edge, or glue a patch of velcro onto the curtain and glue another patch above the stage opening. Lift the curtain up and stick the velcro patches together. The flap curtain can be made out of any kind of fabric; felt is a good choice because it is so durable and easy to work with. Stitch a casing in the top edge of the flap so that the rod will slip through it.

Use the same kind of curtains for smaller stages. Whether you make a tiny finger-puppet box or a large puppet theater, the process is the same. Everyone in the class can make a small finger-puppet stage. Large puppet stages can be used to display student work or to store puppets. They can also be turned into private reading and writing nooks.

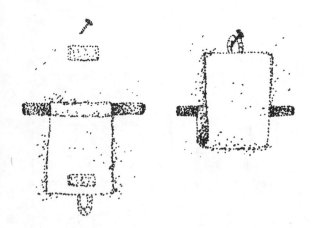

Puppet Tower

Instead of using a large box, make a stage out of a large cardboard barrel. You can make a cardboard barrel out of an appliance box by splitting and rounding it to form a cylindrical shape. Add a fancy cone to turn it into a magical puppet tower. Follow the basic puppet-stage directions on page 72.

Materials:
- large cardboard cylinder
- newspapers
- masking tape
- string and a crayon
- pins
- flour and water
- paint or cloth

Make a pattern for a custom-fitted peaked roof cone by taping newspapers together as illustrated. Tape nine full-size sheets together to form a large square. Find the center of the square by folding the paper in half and in half again. Mark the center point. Then tie a crayon to a piece of string that is 4½′ long. Pin the end of the string to the center of the square. Pull the crayon taut; it should reach the edge of the square. To draw a circle, pull the crayon around the square maintaining the same pressure as you draw. Cut out the circle, taping any loose newspaper edges. Cut a straight line from any point on the circle's edge to the center. Slide one edge over the other to form a cone, or cut the circle in half and slide the cut edges over each other. Hold the cone over the cylinder and adjust the size. Mark the meeting point. If there is a large overlap, cut off some of the excess paper. Use this as a pattern for cutting out cloth or paper. If you decide to make a papier-mâché roof, tape the circle together. Tear 1-2″ strips of newspaper. Mix flour and water into a pancake-batter consistency. Dip the strips of newspaper into the

flour and water; cover the newspaper cone with three or four layers of paper. Paint it with a base coat after it dries. Then decorate it.

This puppet tower could also be a storyteller's tower. Students and teachers climb inside and read or tell stories to the group. Present book reports from this fancy place. Special awards might be given by puppets or people standing in the tower.

Fanciful puppets need fancy stages. They may take a little extra time, but think of the time as a gift to the class. It is a gift of imagination, a statement that tells the students they are worth a special effort. These puppet stages are valuable and versatile teaching props.

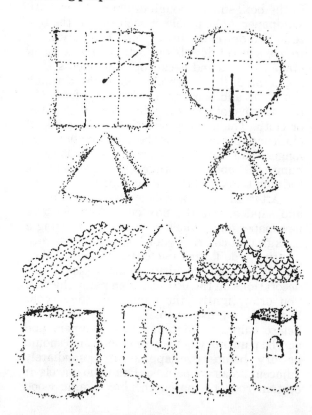

The Walkabout

This puppet stage is in the style of old-fashioned sidewalk placards. Make one out of heavy paper or cardboard tied together with yarn. You can also make one out of cloth, and applique or paint your scenery directly onto the cloth.

The Mouse's House

Set this tiny stage on your lap for a set of finger puppets to inhabit. A shoe box or a deep gift-box in almost any size or shape will do.

Make windows and doors for the puppets to poke through. Cut the openings before you cover the box with paint, cloth, or paper. If you have a plain white box, you can use colored paper to add trim to the house. Make small paper flowers to place in the window boxes. Make the window boxes out of small gift-boxes that have been cut as shown.

For a Victorian shake roof or wall, cut paper into strips of the same width. Scallop or cut peaks in each strip as shown. Glue the first strip at the bottom of the roof with the scalloped edge along the bottom. Glue the next strip over the top of the first strip as shown. Continue to glue strips until you reach the top edge of the roof. Glue the last strip with the scallops or peaks pointing up.

Make other fanciful puppet theaters out of single sheets of colored cardboard. Draw the basic shape of a candy cottage onto a sheet of cardboard. Draw an opening and cut it out with a mat knife or sharp pen knife. Paint colorful pieces of candy on the cottage or cut out paper candy and glue it on the house. Cut a cardboard stand following the directions on page 72.

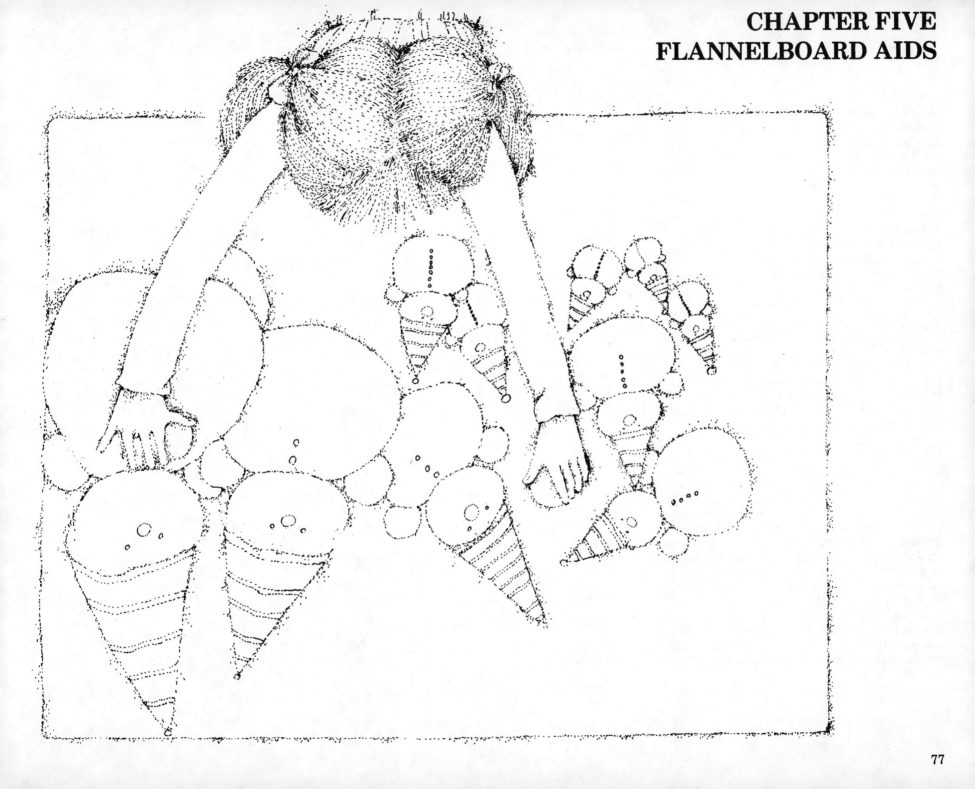

Flannelboard

Traditionally teachers and students have used flannelboards for storytelling, but this medium has many other uses. Flannelboards are ideal for illustrating new ideas and for making cloth murals. Make your flannelboards any size you want. For working with a group, make a 2' x 3' board. For children working alone or in small groups, use 12" x 15" lapboards. You can make a flannelboard book out of five to ten pieces of felt, or you can use the wall to make a giant flannelboard. See the suggestions in chapter 1 for using fabric to cover walls, soundboard, or cardboard panels.

Materials:
- cardboard or acoustic soundboard
- felt or flannel
- scissors
- stapler
- tape
- chalkboard paint, shellac, and brushes (optional)

Use these instructions to make 2' x 3' flannelboards or to make 12" x 15" lapboards. Lapboards with chalkboards on one side are especially useful in small-group teaching. If you want to make a flannelboard chalkboard, use cardboard instead of acoustic soundboard. Paint one side of the cardboard with a coat of shellac. In fifteen minutes paint the cardboard again with a coat of chalkboard paint. Allow the paint to dry for several hours or overnight.

Cut a piece of felt or flannel that is ½" to 1" wider and longer than the board. Then fold the edges of the fabric over the edge of the cardboard, stapling it onto the cardboard. Finish the edges of the board with cloth tape.

Flannelboard Boxes

Make a flannelboard out of one side of a cardboard box. Paint another side of the box with chalkboard paint. Make the third side a puppet stage and the fourth side a pocket chart. Or make a box with a flannelboard on each side, using a different color for each flannelboard.

Flannelboard Book

Materials:
- five to ten 8″ x 10″ rectangular pieces of felt
- velcro
- needle and thread
- assorted trims and colored felt scraps

Sew two or three pieces of velcro on each piece of felt as shown. The velcro will hold flannelboard characters and items in place. Sew or glue a piece of velcro on all items to be used in the book, such as felt numbers and assorted small items. On one page place a felt number. The child chooses that number of items from the assortment you've made and places them next to the number. Also use the book for a classification exercise. Put various shapes, colors, patterns, textures, or paired items in the book and have the students sort these items to match the categories. Use the book to teach sounds or letters to the students. Perhaps you can also use the book to show the sequencing of a progression of figures or shapes from little to big.

Encourage the children to use the book to make up fanciful pictures with felt scraps. If a student makes an unusually nice picture, sew it onto another piece of flannel to take home.

A Giant Flannelboard

Staple or pin felt or flannel onto a wall or bulletin-board. Finish the edges with a border of felt cutouts as illustrated. Changing the border from time to time, use this board to tell stories, to demonstrate concepts with paper or cloth cutouts, or to make a changeable cloth mural. A mural can be a long-term project for the students. Make the background from large pieces of fabric. Make the details and characters from smaller pieces of cloth pinned or sewn together. Use bits of sandpaper glued to the back of paper or cloth cutouts to make the items stick to the flannel.

Use the large board to make two-dimensional designs that the students can duplicate with blocks, or make patterns of shapes and colors for the students to reproduce in other forms.

Use this large flannelboard to create a continuing story. Make basic characters out of felt and glue or sew them together. Add movable parts to the figures. (See page 50.) Have the students make up new adventures for the characters each day. Write out dialogue for the characters on word balloons and pin them above the action.

You can also use the walkabout on page 75 for telling stories. Make it out of several layers of felt or flannel that can be flipped back and forth as the action moves from one scene to another.

Make an accordion-folding flannelboard with a different scene on each section, as shown. As you tell the story, put the characters on one section, folding the other sections out of view.

Scenery

The easiest way to make scenery for your flannelboard is to cut it from felt and sew it to

the background. You can also paint the background with dyes or watercolors; acrylics, oils, and tempera paints will change the texture of the cloth so that the figures don't stick to it well. Dyes can be purchased in small bottles at an art-supply store. The dyes are highly concentrated so that a little goes a long way. Mix three primary colors to make the colors you need.

Another way to make scenery is to stitch the background with thick yarn or crewel yarn. If you don't want to stitch the yarn, pin it onto the board and then pin and glue it in place, removing the pins after the glue dries.

Flannelboard Characters

Make characters out of paper, coloring the figures with marking pens or crayons or painting them. You can also use cutouts from magazines. Make flat paper-figures out of colored construction paper or origami paper. Glue pieces of rough sandpaper onto the backs of the paper characters. The heavier the paper, the more sandpaper you will need to make the paper stick to the flannel. If sandpaper is too costly, make your own by brushing glue onto a sheet of paper and sprinkling sand over the wet glue. Glue scraps of felt or flannel to the back of the paper characters to hold them to the flannelboard.

Pellon is a popular material for flannelboard characters. This material is frequently on sale at fabric shops. Since it is transparent, you can place the pellon over pictures and drawings and trace them onto it quite easily. Then color the figures with marking pens, crayons, or watercolors and cut them out. Pellon sticks to the flannel without sandpaper or felt backing.

Stitch together fancy flannelboard figures from felt scraps and embroidery thread. For someone who enjoys handwork, creating accessories for the flannelboard characters can be an art. Trim the figures with lace, yarn, or braid. Use other kinds of fabric and fake fur for shirts, skirts, and trousers. Fashion animals out of fake fur. Use assorted fabrics to make wardrobes for the flannelboard people. To change characters' roles, you only need to change their costumes. You can also use a key item as a means of identifying characters. For example, turn a girl into Red Riding Hood with a piece of red felt. Place a small wig of yellow yarn on her to create Goldilocks. Use a long wig to make Rapunzel or a nightgown to create Wendy in Peter Pan.

Instead of making one basic set of

characters, you may find it more practical to make a complete set of characters for each story. Keep all the characters for a particular story in one envelope. Some teachers have a file for the poems, stories, and finger plays they do with each class.

Children can make their own flannelboard stories and characters. They can draw them on paper and glue sandpaper on the back.

All children need opportunities to write and illustrate their experiences and fantasies. Years ago Dr. Roach Van Allen promoted and made popular this language-experience philosophy: "What a child does he can talk about. What a child talks about he can write down."

Virginia Gaston, a reading specialist and author, took this idea a step further: "What a child talks about he can write down and illustrate. What a child writes down he can read. And what children write down other children want to read."

Almost everything that children read, listen to, and watch is produced by adults. Naturally the viewpoints are primarily adult. Although children love many wonderful books and films created by adults, it is still important for children to see their own thoughts and ideas come to life and to share this experience with their peers. Part of children's developing sense of worth comes from the way they value their peers. That sense of worth develops with their interest in their peers' experiences and expressions. Nurture this quality in children in the classroom by providing time each day for children to listen to each other, to read each other's work, and to write down and illustrate new ideas and experiences. Have the children write a class newspaper, create class bulletin-boards, and make posters. Encourage them to read aloud to each other, tape-record their stories, and write and illustrate books for other children to read.

Writing and illustrating should occur daily in the classroom. Children can begin by keeping a journal of notes and sketches of things that have happened, things that have been imagined and things they would like to do someday. The daily journal may contain word doodles, picture doodles, fleeting images, puns, jokes, and nonsense. The journals should always be considered private and should only

be shared by children who want to share them. These journals help to establish good writing habits for the children.

Children shyly sharing their work always reminds me of Hughes Mearns' book, *Creative Power: The Education of Youth in the Creative Arts* (2nd ed. rev.—Magnolia, Mass.: Peter Smith Co., 1958). He wrote it in 1929, yet it is a timeless treasure of insights for teachers. He had a drawer in his desk in which children could leave their special work for him to view. The drawer was a private way of sharing children's work and receiving a critique.

Interest children in writing and illustrating their own picture books by asking them to bring some of their favorites from the library or home. Use these books to point out the various parts of a story. Read the story aloud and ask the children to name the main characters. Then ask them to describe:

1. the *setting or location;*

2. the *problem:* man vs. man, man vs. animal, man vs. nature;

3. the *adventure:* development of the problem;

4. the *solution* to the problem.

Go through a number of stories in this way, asking the children to identify the parts of each one.

Write a class story by asking the class or a small group to suggest three or four characters and to describe a location. Then ask someone to suggest a problem. Have the group describe a problem and a solution. Ask each child to make a small illustrated version of the story and then to add captions, either writing them on each page or dictating them to someone else. Children can make story starters for each other. The starters can be exchanged or they can be passed from one person to another with

characters

setting

scenes from the problem and the adventure

solution

three or four different children adding to the story.

Sooner or later someone in the class will want to make a book. Use some favorite books to teach the students the basic parts of a book—the cover, title page, dedication, copyright page, table of contents, chapter headings, index, and information about the author. Ask children to look at an assortment of books and magazines to see how pages are arranged. Point out how the words and pictures are arranged to look attractive.

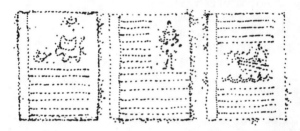

After the children have written their stories, help them to divide it into pages. Have the children look through the story for distinct scenes to illustrate.

Make a set of ditto sheets with lines drawn on them in different arrangements. Place these dittoed sheets underneath a sheet of paper, and the children can use the guide lines as they print the story. These sheets are particularly helpful when children are writing and illustrating books for publication; the lines remind children to stay within the margins so that none of the writing or drawing is lost.

After the story is printed in pencil, go through it with the children to catch any obvious spelling or grammatical errors. This step must be taken with caution and done without discouraging poor spellers and writers from working on books again.

Book Bindings

Teachers or children can do the binding procedures described here, depending on the children's age and ability. Most important for children is the creative act of writing and illustrating their own stories, not assembling and binding the books.

Virginia Gaston and I worked out this basic binding procedure. It is the most durable and long lasting method we have found, and the price is also right.

Materials:
- colored railroad board, lightweight cardboard, or cereal boxes
- paper cutter or heavy-duty scissors
- cloth mystic-tape
- masking tape
- completed story or blank sheets of paper
- stapler
- pencil

Cut two pieces of cardboard 9″ x 11″. One of these pieces will be the front cover and the other the back.

For the front cover, draw a line ½″ from one of the 11″ sides of one piece of cardboard. Cut off the ½″ x 11″ strip.

Then place the ½″ strip next to the side it was cut from, leaving a 1/16″ gap between the two pieces. Tape the strip to the 8½″ x 11″ piece of cardboard, forming a hinge. Without this hinge, the cardboard would snap shut when it was opened. If possible, ask someone to hold the two pieces of cardboard in place while you place a strip of colored mystic-tape over the gap. Take your time; once this tape touches the cardboard, it cannot be moved without ruining both the tape and the board. Start at one end of the tape and press it lightly in place, being careful not to angle the tape off to one side. Or join these two pieces of board with masking tape and save the colored tape for finishing the outside of the book.

Hold the hinged front cover on top of the back cover and trim the extra 1/16″ off the back cover so that both covers are the same size.

Next, cut the story pages or white paper so that it is 8½″ x 11″. Then place the back cover on the table and put the story pages on top of the back cover, lining up the left-hand edges. Now place the hinged cover on top of the story pages on the left side, with the taped side of the hinge against the paper. Put three staples along the ½″ strip as shown. Extra staples will make bumps under the final layer of tape. Cover the staples and the hinge with a piece of colored cloth mystic-tape 1½″ wide. The tape should cover the staples and the 1/16″ gap between the two pieces of board. Use this procedure for any size of book. The only measurement that needs to remain the same is the ½″ width of the hinge strip. Use a ½″ strip for taping and stapling since a narrower strip might tear when it is stapled, and a wider strip will cover up more of the story pages.

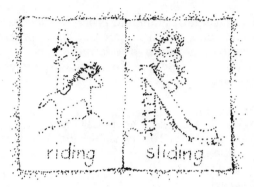

Sometimes you can let the children assemble and bind a book and then write and illustrate the story. For some children the act of binding a book is motivation enough to write a story.

Limit the number of pages in a book to four to six pages. If you make thicker books, most of the pages will be wasted unless you are making a journal. A four- to six-page story will not be as overwhelming for beginning student-authors as ten to twenty pages. With help, even the most reticent author can fill four pages. In some cases the first book may only be a collection of illustrated words or pictures of favorite activities. The next book might contain one sentence on each page. As the author develops confidence and a certain ability to complete a story, however simple, he or she may attempt longer and more complex stories.

To start young children out, small hand-size books containing a few sheets of paper and bound as described can be made ahead of time by aides, volunteers, or older children.

Small Cloth-Bound Books

Here is another binding procedure for making small books. This process is a practical, speedy, inexpensive adaptation of several binding techniques. No special equipment is needed.

Materials:
- cardboard scraps or cereal boxes
- small 5″ x 10″ cloth scraps (avoid polyesters)
- latex glue
- brush
- dish
- ruler, pencil, scrap paper
- paper cutter or heavy-duty scissors
- long-arm stapler or needle and thread

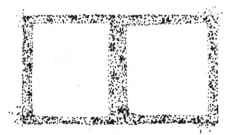

Cut two pieces of 4″ x 4″ cardboard and one piece of 5″ x 10″ cloth. In a dish, mix two tablespoons of glue with two tablespoons of water. Place a piece of waxed paper on the table and put the 5″ x 10″ piece of cloth on the wax paper. Brush the cloth with the glue mixture until the cloth is saturated. Then place the two pieces of cardboard side by side on the cloth with a ½″ margin of cloth around three sides of each square and 1″ between the two squares, as shown.

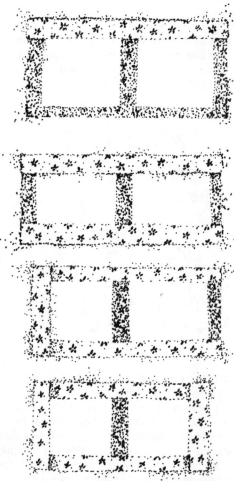

Fold the top edge of fabric over the top of the cardboard, pressing out the wrinkles and pressing the cloth until it sticks to the cardboard. If the material pops up, use a few pins to hold it down while it dries. Turn the bottom edge over; then turn over the two side edges. Leave the cover to dry on the waxed paper or on a plastic surface. When the cloth has dried, peel away the waxed paper. Fold the cover in half so that it forms a book. To make pages, cut 4″ x 8½″ paper rectangles and fold them in

half. Slide the paper inside the cover so that the folded side of the paper touches the inside of the back of the book. With a long-arm stapler fasten the paper to the cover. Instead of stapling, you can sew the paper into the book. Using a needle and heavy-duty thread, sew through the paper and cloth centerfold with a running stitch, as shown.

To finish the book, glue the first page of paper to the inside of the front cover and the last page to the inside of the back cover.

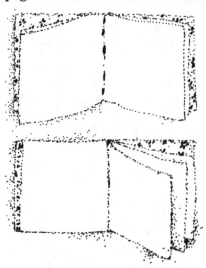

Decorate the cover with yarn, trim, cloth scraps, or colored cloth tape. Cover the stitching or staples with cloth tape.

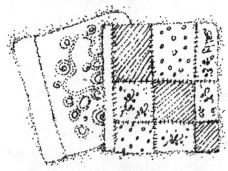

Fingerprint Books

These little books can be used in a number of ways: to make greeting-card books, autograph or phone-number books, recipe books, a holiday treat book, a craft book, a poem, or a songbook.

Materials:
- stamp pads and paper
- fine-point marking pen

Children use their little fingers to print tiny people, bugs, creatures, and plants. To get the children started, ask them to make an illustrated fingerprint tale of a familiar story such as the "Teeny Tiny Woman" or "Thumbelina." Prepare samples to show the children some of the possibilities. For example:
- Mr. Thumb and his matchbox circus
- Tic Tac Toe, a story of ticks and toes
- The inchworm
- Lady bug, lady bug, fly away home
  You might hand out story starters, such as:
- If I were as small as my wee, wee toe, I would . . .
- At first it was a fuzzy fingerprint; then it was a lady bug . . .
- And then it was a teeny tiny woman and her teeny tiny man . . .
- And then it was . . .

Once children get the idea, ask them to invent their own tiny characters and create original stories.

Shape Books

The shapes of books interest children in writing and reading them. This shape-book format is a good one for science reports and for creative writing. Encourage children to make their own shape patterns, first sketching a shape and then cutting it out and using it as a pattern for the cover and pages.

There are obvious shapes, like an Easter-egg book containing a story for the Easter holiday. An egg-shaped book might be a science study with each page devoted to an animal that comes from an egg. An egg-shaped book could also be filled with egg recipes, stories about chickens, or the life story of one chicken from egg to hen or rooster. It might be a book of colorful Easter-egg decorations. Each page of the book could feature a design from a different culture.

These shapes can also be used to make interesting books: shoe, foot, moon, sun, stars, egg, leaf, blossom, mouse, cat, bunny, tree, bell, bird, alligator, car, bus, plane, or rainbow. The "At first it was . . ." idea, described with the fingerprint books, can be used for story starters with these books too.

Adapt the following popular game for shape-book writing. The game starts with a sentence such as, "My Aunt Matilda asked me to come and visit her, so I packed my suitcase and in it I put my alligator bag. . . ." Each person repeats the sentence, adding a new item that starts with the next letter of the alphabet (bon-bons, a cap, dungarees). Each time the game is played, different criteria are used for the items—in one game only ridiculous items can be packed, and in another game only edible items.

To adapt the game to a book, children can make a suitcase-shaped book and draw each item on a different page. One suitcase book might contain only items to take on a space trip, and another one might show the things needed on a safari or circus trip, or things a city mouse would take on a trip to the country.

Fill a stocking-shaped book with drawings and descriptions of all the things a wonderful Christmas stocking can hold. Use a shoe-shaped book to show a collection of shoes for every occasion and to give a history of shoes. A shoe book could also be filled with designs for silly shoes, such as shoes for elephants who roller skate, shoes for a spider or rubber boots for an ostrich.

TALL TALES

short stories

in tiny shape books

slide small books into a pocket

A Real Egg Story

So far the books mentioned look like books. Each has a front cover and a back cover and pages in between. Books can be made in other shapes and out of less traditional materials. Consider an egg story coming out of an egg—a real egg, a plastic egg container, or a cardboard Easter egg. Kim Hansen, a friend of mine, gave me an egg saga written on yards of tickertape rolled up in five nested eggs; each part of the story was placed in one of the eggs.

Use a very large egg container to hold an assortment of egg-shaped pieces of paper and cloth that could be played with and arranged into designs. This egg container could be a movable collage book. Some of the eggs might have egg-related words printed on them so that the collage could be an egg story as well. Blank, laminated egg shapes could be included for children to write words on.

Use fingernail scissors to cut a ½" hole in the top of an egg; it may take several eggs to do this successfully. Empty the egg into a dish and save it for an omelet. Have children write letters, poems, or short stories on paper that is small enough to fit into the opening in the egg. Roll or fold the paper into a shape small enough to pass through the ½" hole in the egg. When the paper is in the egg, cut a 1" square out of white paper or cloth. Try to glue the square to the inside of the hole by wetting the cloth with glue, pushing it into the hole with a toothpick, and pressing it against the edges of the hole. Glue the cutout piece of egg over the hole, and the egg should look almost new again. Decorate the egg with colored pens, paper, or stickers. Don't submerge the egg in dye because the dye will probably leak inside, but the egg could be dyed before the hole is cut.

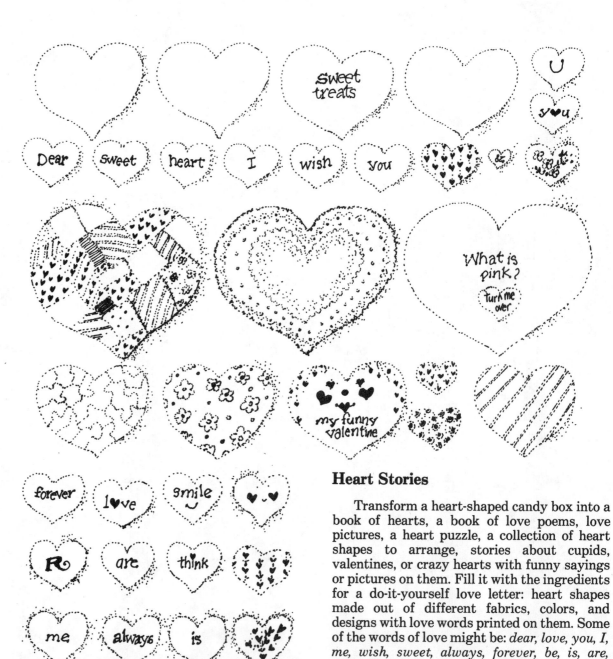

Heart Stories

Transform a heart-shaped candy box into a book of hearts, a book of love poems, love pictures, a heart puzzle, a collection of heart shapes to arrange, stories about cupids, valentines, or crazy hearts with funny sayings or pictures on them. Fill it with the ingredients for a do-it-yourself love letter: heart shapes made out of different fabrics, colors, and designs with love words printed on them. Some of the words of love might be: *dear, love, you, I, me, wish, sweet, always, forever, be, is, are, smile, flowers, think.*

Rebus Books

Use a stamp set made from erasers or art foam to make a set of characters, basic props, and scenery for your rebus. Some possible rebus items are flowers, trees, animals, and symbols for words used in rebuses, such as eye, four, or R. Children can use the stamps to write and illustrate their own stories.

95

The Unending Tale
(A Moebius-Strip Book)

A moebius strip is a one-sided, continuous surface attached at both ends.

Materials:
- colored construction paper
- scissors
- glue or tape
- pens

To make a moebius strip, cut a 3″ x 12″ piece of paper. Draw a line down the center of the strip. Then hold the strip and twist one end before taping the two ends together. Pierce the center of the strip and cut along the center line. Continue to cut until you come to the place where you began. You now have a large ring instead of two separate rings. Place your finger on one side of the strip and run it along the surface of the paper. You will find that the ring has only one surface. Have the children start at any point on the surface and write a story that goes on and on. Use the circles on the facing page as story starters.

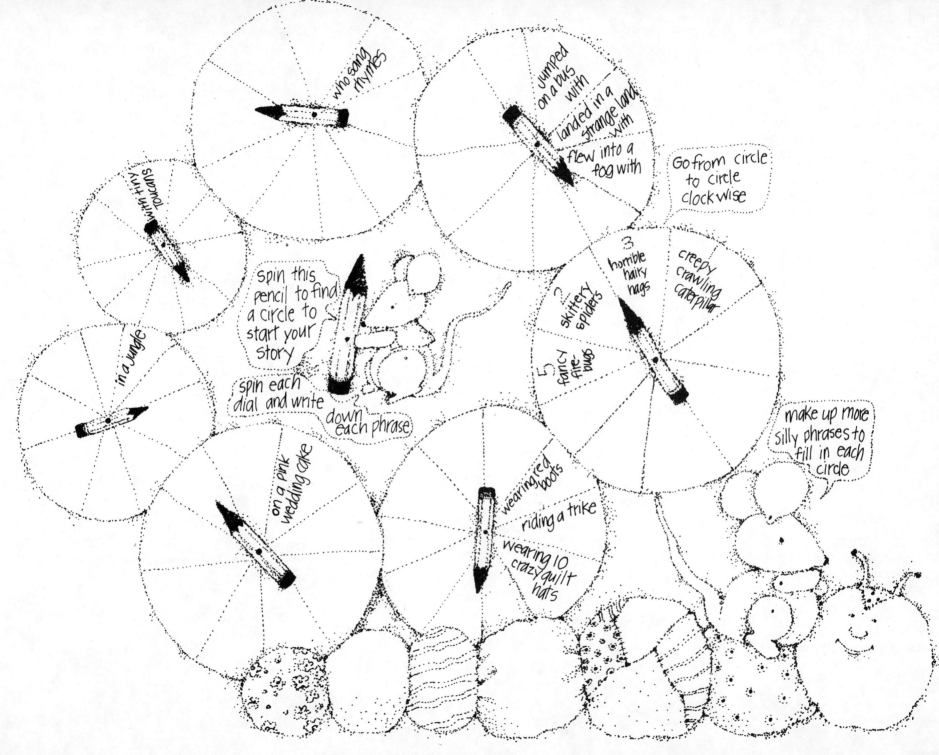

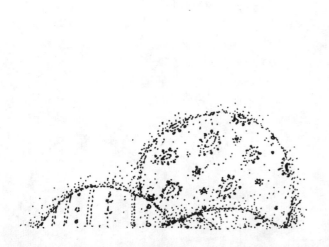

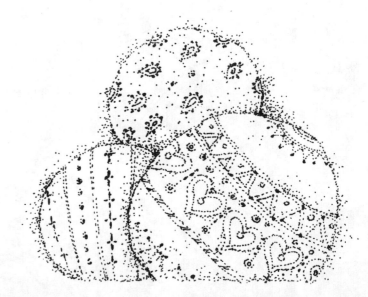

Not all the most worthwhile art experiences happen in thirty or even sixty minutes. Children need ample time to discover the properties and possibilities of different materials. They need to work with materials alone, in small groups, and in large groups. Long-term art projects are a way to help children develop sustained concentration over a long period of time. They may learn that, even in a project they like, a certain amount of relatively boring or rote activity goes toward the final result. By doing a long-term project, children learn to plan, to obtain materials, and to sequence tasks. They will also discover the rewards of working together.

These projects also help the classroom in other positive ways. A long-term project can be used to bring the class down to earth on wild days by focusing energies on a familiar activity. Certainly the final result of a project will become a part of the class memory.

To choose a long-term project, consider what you can handle with the materials you already have or with those materials you can easily obtain. Present three possible projects to the children and let them choose which one they'd like to do. Let the children figure out what they will need for the project, plan the steps needed to complete it, and choose the parts of the project they would like to do.

If the project is a well-planned and quiet activity, some children can work at it during music or reading periods. Some projects can be done to the accompaniment of music, or children might listen to a story while they stitch, hook a rug, work with clay, or weave.

Give the finished product to the school or to a library, children's hospital, nursery school, or park. You might start an art-lending library, or you could sell the finished project at an auction and use the proceeds for a class celebration or for special materials or equipment for the class or school.

It's important to remember that the value of a long-term project is in the group cooperation, the dynamics of the whole operation, not solely in the outcome. The finished product is important to the children, but the knowledge learned through the activity is more important. If the children are given the proper materials and enough time to work with them, the result will be satisfactory.

Your expectations will affect the result. If you understand and appreciate what children are capable of at the various stages of development and don't impose adult standards on the children's efforts, the project will be a success. Expect the activity to be wonderful and it will be. Here are some suggested themes for the long-term projects described in this chapter:

- a zoo
- favorite playthings
- sports
- animals and their young
- Noah's ark

Paint a Mural
Indoors or Outdoors

First, have the class choose a theme and figure out what they want to illustrate. Then have students design a mural for this theme by any one of the following methods:

1. Have everyone in the class draw a mural on paper; vote on the one mural they want to paint.

2. Have everyone in the class design a section of the mural. Each child does a certain thing. For example, one child does the ground, and others do the sky, trees, flowers, insects, houses, animals, or automobiles.

3. Have each child design an assigned or chosen area.

If a few children design it, the rest of the children can do other tasks—some paint, some mix, some clean up.

Once you've chosen the mural design and the method you're going to use, redraw the design on a larger scale on newspapers or butcher paper. Cut out some and use them as patterns.

Wipe all the dust and grease off the wall or surface to be painted, cover any woodwork with masking tape, and tape newspapers and plastic drop cloths over the floor beneath the wall.

Cut some cardboard boxes down to 5″ high. Set paint containers in these to keep paint from spilling all over the floor if the paint is knocked over.

Sketch the main outline mural with chalk or light pencil. First paint the large background areas—the sky, ground, and grass—allowing each area to dry thoroughly before painting adjacent areas. If you're painting the mural near the classroom, it's better to paint one color at a time. This will force children to let the painted areas dry completely before they add more details. However, there are times when a mural is painted in another location and must be completed in a day or two. Acrylic and latex paints will dry in ten to thirty minutes, but enamels will take twelve hours or more to dry completely.

Tile Mural

Materials:
- paper squares
- pencil
- crayons or marking pens
- turpentine
- ceramic tiles in plain colors
- enamel paints
- brushes

Decide whether the overall design will be large, covering many little squares, or whether it will be made of individually designed small squares.

Cut squares of paper in the same size as the tiles and draw designs on them. Then assemble the squares into a mural and color the designs with marking pens or crayons. You can tape or staple the individual squares on a long piece of butcher paper. When you have arranged the squares, number them in order. Then assign a section or a color to each child. Show the children how to work together on similar sections or with the same colors.

For a variation of this method, you can draw a mural on a large piece of butcher paper. First mark the paper off into squares that are the same size as the tile. Number each of the squares and draw designs on them. Then cut the squares apart and distribute them.

Brush a bit of turpentine onto each tile and let the tile become sticky. Use a pencil to copy the design on the paper square onto the tile. Let the turpentine dry. Then paint the design with enamel paint and place it in a preheated oven at 350° for twenty minutes.

When all the tiles are painted, apply them to the surface you wish to cover, following the grouting directions on the grout package.

Papier-Mâché Projects

Make life-size papier-mâché figures or animals. For this project, you might want to work in small groups of three to four children for each figure.

Materials:
- chicken wire
- wire cutter
- gloves
- newspapers
- flour and water, wheat paste, or white glue
- masking tape
- sandpaper
- white latex or gesso paint

Wearing gloves and using wire cutters, work the chicken wire into the shape you want. With the wire cutter, twist the cut ends together to join parts of the figure. You can also use a thin wire to tie the chicken wire together.

To begin the papier-mâché, use masking tape to attach large 5″ wide strips of newspaper around the figure. This creates a surface to stick wet strips of newspaper onto. Dip 1-2″ wide strips of newspaper into flour and water or wheat paste and press the wet strips over the frame. Continue to add strips until you have covered the wire with a ½″ layer of newspapers. To create a smooth surface, completely cover the figure with small 1″ x 1″ squares or with torn circles of newspaper, carefully pressing the edges down. Run your fingers over the surface pressing down any rough edges. Then allow the paper to dry thoroughly. Sand away any rough spots.

Add small features such as ears, nose, or muscles by making small wads of newspaper. Tape them on to the basic shape with strips of glue-soaked newspaper, smoothing the strips over the features. Add more wads and strips if the features are not large enough.

To add texture and detail to the figure before painting, try gluing items like these to the surface: rice, assorted pasta, buttons, thin rolls of newspaper, glass beads, papier-mâché beads, and small shapes made out of papier-mâché. Paper pulp is another way to add texture. Soak paper in water until it falls apart, squeeze the water out, and shape it in beads or whatever small shapes you want. Then moisten the outside surface with glue or wheat paste before you press the paper-pulp shapes to the surface.

After everything is dry, paint the entire figure with a white latex or gesso base coat. After this coat dries, paint the basic background colors, let the paint dry, and then paint in the details. Paint the entire figure with several coats of clear plastic or lacquer in a matte or gloss finish.

Classroom Friendship Quilt

This early American tradition is an excellent activity for children to do as you read aloud to them. Initially each child in the class makes a square or portion of the quilt. Then all of the fabric is quilted.

Materials:
- scrap paper
- pencils and crayons
- construction paper
- tissue paper or tracing paper
- needle and thread
- scissors
- cloth scraps
- quilt backing
- a sheet of batting in the size of the quilt
- quilting frame
- sewing machine (optional)

Introduce themes for the quilt design and have the class choose one. Some of the possible themes are: a spring garden, baby animals, what we did this year, historical events, self-portraits, or the alphabet.

Have each child design and color a square. For a more coordinated color scheme, have children design their squares first, arrange them together, and then choose an overall color scheme for the entire quilt.

On a large table or bulletin board, have several children make a design by arranging the squares and strips of colored paper to represent borders. Have the other children comment on and make changes in the design, choosing the best location for each square. Next, decide what background color to use for each square. Give each child cloth for the background of his or her square.

Make a pattern with tissue or tracing paper for each part of the design. Cut out the design parts and put the patterns on top of cloth scraps. Pin each pattern piece and cut ¼″ away from the pattern to allow for a ¼″ hem.

Pin the fabric cutouts onto the background cloth. Show the students how to do these stitches to appliqué their designs onto the squares: blanket stitch, hidden stitch, simple stitch, small stitch, and running stitch.

After each child has completed a square, arrange all the parts on a table. Pin and baste all the parts together. Use a machine to stitch the squares together, or have children stitch the squares together by hand. Place the pieced quilt on top of the batting and the quilt backing. Then baste the quilt sandwich together to keep the layers from slipping as you quilt it.

Show children samples of quilting methods to help them decide which one to use. Then put the quilt on a frame or on a large quilting hoop, and show the children how to quilt it. Schedule small groups to work on a quilting bee. As a part of the quilting design, have the children stitch their signatures in the borders around their own squares.

Painted Quilt

Materials:
- squares of cloth
- pencil
- acrylic paints
- brushes

Have the children design quilt squares and lightly pencil the designs onto the squares. Paint the squares, letting the paint dry thoroughly before painting adjacent areas. Test the paint on cloth scraps to see that it's not too thick or too thin.

After the design is completely painted and dried, stitch the painted squares together. Baste the pieced quilt, batting, and backing together and quilt it along the design lines.

Animated Films

Use these introductory activities to teach the basic principles of animation. Beginning animation projects make good learning-center activities.

Flip Books

Cut twenty-five 2″ x 3″ pieces of paper. Staple the pieces together at one end and draw a dot or a simple figure on the first piece or page. On the next page draw an identical dot ¼″ away from the position of the dot on the first page. On the third page, draw another dot, moving it over another ¼″. Draw a dot on each page, moving it ¼″ from the position of the last dot. Then flip the pages and watch the dot move. A flip book demonstrates the process used to make an animated film.

Try the same idea with a figure such as the silly clown shown. Draw his eyes moving back and forth, or draw his arms waving and his legs kicking.

You can also do a collage project for a flip book. Cut 4″ x 5″ pieces of paper and staple them together on one end. Cut twenty-five identical shapes out of colored paper, making them small enough to fit on the 4″ x 5″ pages. Glue one shape on each page, positioning them so that they will move in the following ways when the pages are flipped.

- zigzag
- turn in circles
- appear in one corner after another
- run around the edge of the paper
- point in one direction and then in the other direction
- spin
- jump up and down

Choose a theme, such as favorite foods for another flip book. On the last page of the book, draw a person sitting at a table, with his or her mouth open. Cut out magazine pictures of food and glue them on the pages so that when the pages are flipped, favorite foods will appear, land on a table, and then go into the person's mouth. To show the person eating one type of food, draw the same food on each page, each

Arrange clowns and other circus figures on the background before shooting each child's clown in action

time making the drawing smaller so it will look as if the person is taking bites of the food.

You don't need to invest much money in using flip books to teach children the basics of animation. However, if you want to teach them about movies, you'll need to use a movie camera.

Movies

Materials:
- paper
- construction paper
- scissors
- Super-8 camera with single-frame switch
- Super-8 film in 50' cartridges
- stand to hold camera tripod
- light for indoor shooting
- projector or film loop
- splicer

Make a larger version of the moving clown used in the flip-book activity. Using construction paper, first cut a background piece that is the same proportion as a frame of movie film.

Have each child make a clown out of pieces of colored paper. Place the clown on the background paper, but don't glue it down.

The animation takes place as the children move a part of the clown's body, take a single frame, and then move the clown again. They repeat this over and over again until the action or movement is completely filmed. Soon the children will get an idea of how much movement should be made from frame to frame to create smooth transitions.

For a variation of this project, shoot pictures of clay figures in a diorama. Children move the arms of each clay figure, changing the figure's position before each shot.

Shoot an inanimate object, such as a toy car moving down a road in a town made of blocks, or shoot a doll or stuffed animal in a doll house.

For another variation, shoot a fantasy film. Choose a theme such as funny zoo heroes or outerspace fantasy characters.

Decide whether to make a face or full-figure shot. Children draw their own characters and choose one or two parts of the character's body to animate. Obvious parts such as eyes, arms, and mouths are good for beginners to start with. However, there are a lot of other possibilities—a mustache that curls and uncurls, eyebrows, a bow tie that flips, a thumping heart, or toes that curl up at the ends.

If you have a 50′ cartridge, you'll have 2½ minutes of film. Determine the number of frames needed for the title and the credits, and then divide the rest of the frames among the characters. Before filming, have children practice the movements their characters will make in each frame.

Film an animated drawing as another rather quick group film-project. Choose a theme, such as children around the world or the alphabet (letters or animals, food, and nonsense words in alphabetical order).

Begin drawing and take a one or two frame shot of the drawing as it progresses. First have the children sketch what they are going to draw. Have them practice drawing it in a given number of shots, such as eighteen two-frame shots—or eighteen moves for each character.

Write the title and credits a few letters at a time.

After everyone has mastered the basic animation techniques and knows how to figure out movement and timing, it's time to consider a longer animation project. They might film favorite stories or stories they have written.

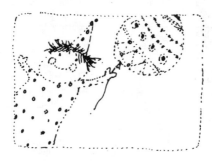

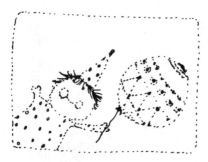

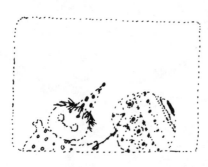

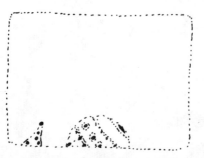

Consider making films of subjects the students are studying.

Break the class into production teams of artists, writers, camera people, editors, designers, and title artists. For these projects, children will need to make storyboards (see page 107), and they'll need to plan and make a chart showing who does what and when. For elaborate films, the artists may need help in painting and creating the frames.

Once work is underway, delegate some of the artwork to members of the class to work on during free times.

In some situations try to have one or several children assume the position of art director, and have them assign art to the children in the class who are particularly interested in drawing buildings, flowers, horses, or whatever is needed.

Primarily I have written about the visual aspect of film, but sound is also an essential part. It might only be a track of music, but choosing the music to fit the art is important and can bring out the best in a film. You'll need a good tape recorder and a source of music. Work with the children in choosing the music and use a local or school library for reference books.

When everything is ready, shoot the film. Some films will take more time than others to shoot, especially if cut out pieces of paper are manipulated on a background. Careful film planning will eliminate the need for much editing in animated films. However, editing and some of the other technical aspects of filmmaking are not nearly as difficult as some people think. Ask a local media specialist or someone at a camera shop to help you. Perhaps a shop will loan you a splicer. Once you have made the film, you can have it put in a film-loop cassette.

Storyboards

This story-planning method is useful in planning filmstrips as well as films, both live-action and animated.

Materials:
- cardboard
- scissors
- 18″ x 24″ sheets of construction paper
- colored fine-point pens
- pencils
- scrap paper

To introduce the storyboard idea, draw a set of TV screens on a chalkboard, or cut out some large screens to pin on a board. Ask the class to help you retell a familiar story, and ask children to draw a picture and a caption in each frame.

To make storyboards, draw a smaller screen on a piece of cardboard and cut it out. Use the cutout cardboard as a pattern to draw frames on an 18″ x 24″ sheet of construction paper.

On an 18″ x 24″ sheet, you can trace a 4″ x 5″ screen to make three rows of four frames as shown, or use a 3″ x 4″ screen and get five rows of frames. Children illustrate stories on the storyboards, writing captions in the frames. The screens can also be drawn on individual pieces of scrap paper. The scrap-paper screens can be cut out and glued onto the construction paper, or they can be shifted around, as shown, while the students plan their stories.

Changes can be made on the storyboards by drawing screens on scratch paper and gluing them over the screen that is to be replaced, or children can cut out the screens on the storyboard and rearrange them on another sheet of construction paper.

Recognizing children's efforts and achievements is an important part of a creative classroom. Even those children who find gratification in new knowledge or skills enjoy some recognition. For many other children, recognition motivates them to learn.

Recognition can be as simple as putting children's work on display. You can also ask children to demonstrate their skills to the class or to a gathering of students and parents.

An Honorary Hat

Use this hat on special occasions. You may want to rotate its use daily or weekly. Privileges, such as being the snack cook for the day, receiving an extra choice in a game, or having a special time with the teacher, go along with the hat.

Materials:
- assorted trims
- embroidery thread
- needle and thread
- scissors
- felt or a purchased hat

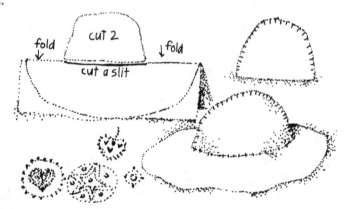

Try to reward children in ways that don't encourage them to compete with each other. Reduce peer competition by encouraging students to compete with their own records or previous achievements and by recognizing personal improvement and originality as well as skill. You can also use rewards and recognitions to show children that each person has a set of special skills and talents to offer to the group. In this way, children will learn to enjoy giving recognition as well as receiving it.

The items described in this chapter can be used to reward or recognize children in your classroom or other special people.

Make the hat yourself and ask each child to contribute an item to sew on it. Add fanciful items constructed from scraps and trims to the hat to make it more festive.

Ask each child to make a small ornament less than 2″ wide or 2″ high for the hat. Make ornaments from cloth or paper. You may want to draw or sew words and designs on them. Make appliquéd badges, embroidered patches, or small stuffed figures or animals to hang on the hat. The directions on page 64 might be helpful to the children as they make ornaments for the hat.

A Special Necklace

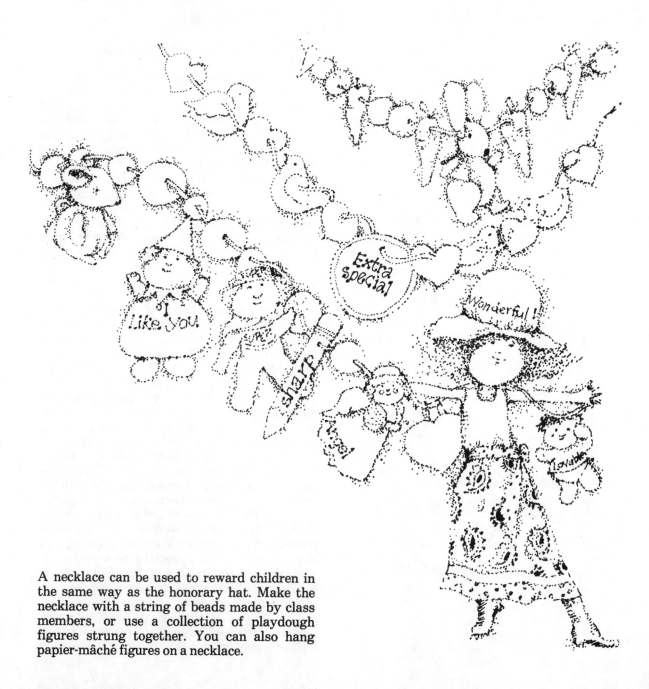

A necklace can be used to reward children in the same way as the honorary hat. Make the necklace with a string of beads made by class members, or use a collection of playdough figures strung together. You can also hang papier-mâché figures on a necklace.

Green and Growing Awards

Make garlands of flowers to wear on the head or around the neck. Bestow these awards on birthdays or other special occasions. Make them as awards for special guests.

Materials:
- flowers or colored tissue paper
- scissors
- florist wire
- pins
- paper doilies
- ribbon

Cut the stem of the flower off 1″ below the blossom. Insert thin florist wire up the stem and through the blossom. Then turn the end of the wire into a hook and gently pull it back into the blossom. Wire a bunch of flowers in this way and tie them together into a small bouquet. Wrap a piece of wire around sprigs of fern and greenery to include greenery in the bouquet.

Join one or two flowers to make a small corsage or string flowers on a wire. Twist greens and blossoms into a crown.

If you can't obtain real flowers, make some out of colored tissue paper. To make flowers, cut any of the flower shapes shown out of tissue paper. Take three or four paper blossoms and pinch the centers together. Twist wire or tape around the centers to hold the blossoms together. Peel each piece of paper back and shape it into a petal arrangement. To make a bouquet, twist a number of these blossoms together. Then add some real greens and poke the bunch through a paper doily. Wrap florist tape around the neck of the bouquet and tie a ribbon around it.

The Fairy Godmother

Make a life-size, desk-size, or hand-size fairy godmother. Sit the figure in a rocking chair in the reading corner or with a different group of children each hour or day. Let the fairy godmother grace a cafeteria table to remind the children to behave themselves during lunch. She can even sit in the teacher's chair. Turn her into Mother Goose, Mother Nature, Mrs. Claus, a pilgrim, or a fairy queen with a change of clothes. Reward some children with the task of costuming her. Let the fairy godmother preside over special celebrations.

Materials:
- butcher paper or newspapers
- pencil
- scissors
- old bedsheet or large piece of skin-colored cloth
- sewing machine
- pins, needle, and thread
- polyester stuffing or old stockings
- embroidery thread or marking pens that won't bleed on cloth
- yarn and assorted decorative trims

Ask a child to lie down on a large piece of butcher paper or on two pieces of newspaper. Trace around the child. Then cut out the pattern you've traced and pin it onto a double thickness of cloth. Cut around the pattern and then remove the pattern from the cloth. Pin the right sides of the cloth pieces together and sew a seam ½″ from the edge, leaving a 10″ opening on one side of the torso. To turn the material right side out, pull the cloth through the opening. Then put stuffing into the opening, filling the legs first. Push the stuffing down into the toes, feet, and lower legs. Stuff the arms and head next. The stuffing will shape the body. The way the stuffing is pushed into the material and the amount of stuffing

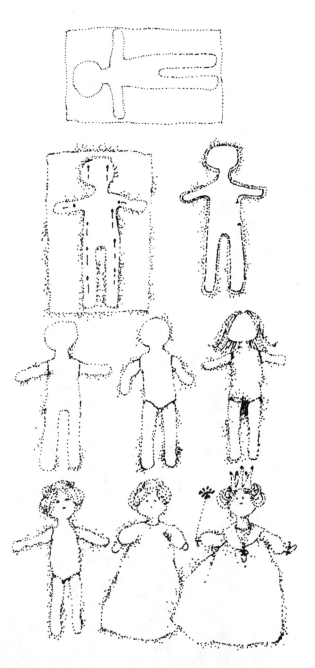

used can change the shape of the parts of the body.

After the arms, legs, and head are stuffed, sew across the tops of the arms and legs, as shown. The stitching in these four spots will help the arms and legs bend easily. Finally, stuff the torso and then hand-stitch the opening shut. If you want a matronly fairy godmother, sew a set of small cushions onto her chest or put extra stuffing into her upper torso. Embroider or draw on facial features, or glue on felt cutouts for the eyes, nose, mouth, and cheeks. Make a yarn wig following the directions on page 68. Dress the finished figure in cast-off or thrift-store clothes.

Variations

Make a simple version of this life-size doll out of old nylon stockings. Three or four pairs of pantyhose will be enough. Stuff one pair with polyester stuffing. Then stuff a pair of nylons that have been cut off just below the knees as shown. Sew the cut end shut. Then stitch the waists together, leaving an opening so that you can stuff the torso of the body. Cut one leg off a third pair of stockings to make the head. Tie or sew one end of the thigh section shut and stuff it. Make facial features on the figure following the directions on page 68. Then tie the neck together and sew it onto the body as shown. Sew on a yarn wig and dress the figure.

Turn the fairy godmother into a giant pocket-lady, peddler woman, or "Katy-no-pockets" by making an apron and sewing lots of pockets on it. Put a special note, award, task card, or message in each pocket. Fill some of her pockets with coupons good for certain activities or privileges. You can draw a basic coupon on a ditto master and make as many copies as you need. Make a male version in the form of a popular story character or folk hero.

Oscar

Oscar is a round tube of fake fur stuffed with cloth scraps or old stockings. Make a small version that lives in a soup can or a full-size one who lives in a regular trash can. Use Oscar in the same way as the fairy godmother is used.

Materials:
- 8½" x 11" paper or newspapers
- pencil
- scissors
- pins
- one large piece and extra scraps of green fake fur, velour, or felt
- sewing machine
- needle and thread
- buttons
- stuffing
- soup or trash can
- paint and brush

Draw a large worm shape on a newspaper or a small worm shape on a piece of 8½" x 11" paper. Cut out the pattern and pin it onto a double thickness of fake fur turned inside out. Cut your pattern out and then stitch the tube about ½" from the edge, leaving one end open for stuffing. Turn the tube right side out and stuff it. Stitch the open end and sew on eyes made of buttons and a mouth. Stick your Oscar figure in a can so that his head peeks out. Paint "Oscar" on the side of the can or on a paper taped to a toothpick or dowel. Crumple up some scraps of paper "trash" and put the scraps in the can with Oscar to make him feel comfortable.

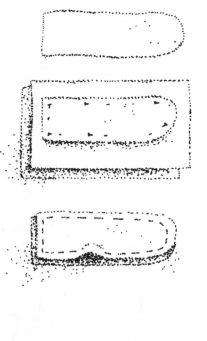

Superhearts

Cut out a large cardboard heart shape and write "Superheart" on it as shown. Color the heart with marking pens or paint and cover it with laminating film or clear contact paper. Glue or tape a pin-back on it, or punch a hole and thread a string through the hole to make a necklace.

Make felt superhearts by cutting out two felt hearts. Sew felt cutout letters and decorations on one heart. Sew the decorated heart and the plain heart together and stuff them. Sew a safety pin to the back. Make hearts that are small and delicate or very large (10-12" across). Have the children make superhearts to give to classroom volunteers at the end of the year. Give a superheart to a class member who has done something special.

Stuffed Initials

Draw letters or words on paper, overlapping the letters as shown. Cut out a letter or word. Then pin the pattern onto a double thickness of cloth and cut it out. Blanket stitch the edges together and stuff the letter or word. Hang the stuffed item on a ribbon that's long enough to slip over someone's head.

Use this method to make a stuffed banana and embroider "Top Banana" on it, or make a stuffed wedge of cheese with the words "Big Cheese" on it.

Purple Cows

Present this award for original art work and for experimenting with new ways to handle familiar materials. Reward effort, experimentation, and even failures rather than finished products. Children need to be encouraged to pursue the process and to worry less about the results when they first learn a new technique or use a new material.

Draw a cow on cardboard and paint it purple, or make a cow out of purple felt. Sew a pin on the back of it. Decorate the cow outlandishly. Let children who earn the purple-cow award wear the pin for a day.

Play-Dough Awards

To make an award out of play dough, mix one cup of salt with four cups of flour. Add water and mix it with your hands until the dough holds together without feeling sticky. Knead the dough until it becomes smooth and shiny, kneading in dabs of paint for color; you can also paint the dough after it's baked. Roll or shape the dough, using a garlic press and toothpicks to add details to the awards. Bake them in a 350° oven for fifteen to sixty minutes, checking the oven frequently to make sure the dough isn't overbaking. You can also use commercial oven-baked dough from a hobby store.

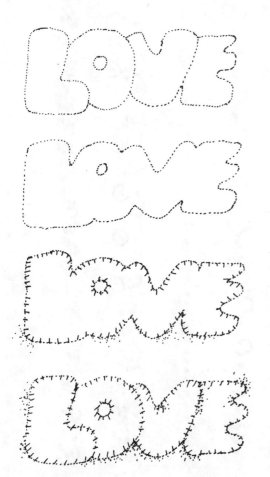

Official Documents

Design your own fancy certificates and contracts for the children, and have children help you design and make awards for classroom volunteers and aides.

Materials:
- white paper
- scratch paper
- pencil
- black fine-point pens
- rubber stamps and stamp pad
- stickers, decorations, and ribbons
- rubber cement
- press-on letters and designs (optional)

It's always possible to buy blank certificates at a stationery store, but it's more fun to use certificates that have a personal quality or are designed for a particular achievement.

Design a few basic certificates that can be used for many purposes, leaving blanks for words and decorations. Before you sketch ideas for certificates, decide on the wording. Next, decide on the borders and themes. Art-supply stores have a selection of press-on borders and designs. You may want to look at some of these to get ideas. Try making your own borders; they're not as complicated as they look. Start with a scallop design as shown. Add a circle, some dots, and a few leaves. Practice making a variety of borders. You might cut a design on a rubber eraser (page 32) and stamp it over and over around the certificate, or use several stamps to make a border.

To write on the certificates, use letter stamps (page 33), press-on letters, or fancy pen-and-ink lettering. Decorate the certificates with official-looking stickers and ribbons. Glue parts of the certificate on with dabs of rubber cement, rubbing off the excess cement after it dries.

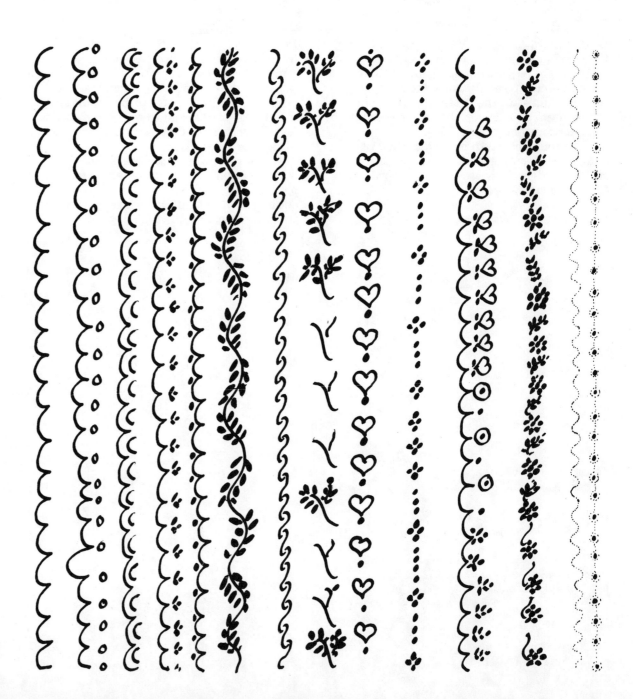

Once you've designed a basic certificate, make photocopies of it. A photocopy can be used to make a mimeograph stencil if you want even more copies. An instant printing service will make copies quickly and relatively inexpensively.

To prepare art for printing, use the following rules. Leave a ½″ margin around the edges of an 8½″ x 11″ sheet of paper to give the printer or mimeograph space for handling it. Expensive printing jobs can accommodate art that bleeds off the page, but for school printing this isn't practical.

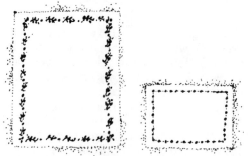

Make the certificates on white paper. Do your lettering in black ink; some blue inks will not show up on a reproduction. At an art store, buy a non-repro blue pencil and use it to sketch and draw the lines on the original. Then do the actual drawing and lettering in black ink.

Most inexpensive printing processes won't reproduce large solid black areas well. Keep solid areas or large letters under ¼″ thick. Instead of drawing solid areas with solid lines, use a pattern of black dots or lines.

When you are ready to award certificates, put the children's names on them with fancy pen-and-ink lettering, press-on letters, or letter stamps.

Try using calligraphy to make official-looking certificates. Look for books on calligraphy at the library, and buy a special pen and nibs at an art store.

Calligraphy

Materials:
- waterbase calligraphy ink
- pen, holder, and nibs
- white paper
- vellum or parchment
- opaque correction fluid

The key word about calligraphy is *practice*. The more you do, the better you become. There is no shortcut to a good calligraphy technique.

Practice the following strokes until you can do them easily and smoothly. As you practice you will learn to judge how much ink is in the pen and how much you need to blot the nib before writing with it.

To learn an alphabet you must use a guide sheet of letters for at least twenty hours of practice. After that, take the guide out for reference but use it less frequently. Twenty hours sounds like a long time, but it's only one hour a day for less than a month. Every time you need to write something, practice your calligraphy. Do it while you are listening to TV, radio, or records. Practice on your lunch breaks. Address your Christmas cards early, practicing with the small nibs that can be used for writing letters. Use calligraphy to make grocery lists, pay the bills, make lesson plans, and write notes or cards. Write out your favorite poems. Practice writing vocabulary for a foreign language. Taking a calligraphy class may help you to practice, but you may want to do the practicing on your own.

Once you learn one alphabet style, you'll find you can learn a second alphabet much faster. Be a perfectionist only if you have time—many people spoil art experiences for themselves by not being satisfied with their own efforts. The fact that you did it yourself will mean more to your students and friends than the quality of the product.

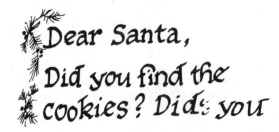

She sells seashells
pink pulpy pickles
the fat cat sat and
Joy Smiles Sweet

Grocery List

milk — JUICE
butter — TEA
cheese — FISH
bread
crackers — flowers
sour cream — peanut butter / salt / baking powder
cereal
lettuce — apples
cabbage — oranges
onions — peaches
raisins — nuts

Of course you want to achieve a nice balance and make something that looks attractive and neat. Correct spelling errors, and don't leave big splatters of ink or dirty fingerprints all over your work.

Dear Santa,
Did you find the
cookies? Did you

Some errors and dirty marks can be covered up with an opaque correction fluid. This correction fluid won't look good on an actual certificate, but it works well on art that is going to be printed or photocopied. Write the correct letter on top of the mistake and then white out the portions of the first letter that are still visible. You may want to white out the mistake completely. Then draw a new letter on a piece of paper, cut out the paper, and glue it over the error.

Here are some sample certificates, several of them including art done by children. Using children's art is especially nice for certificates that go to parents and adults.

Thank You!

to ....

for ....

To ....

in

Appreciation

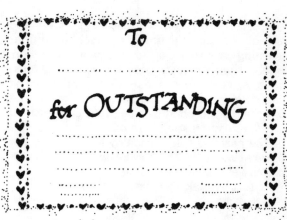

To ....

for OUTSTANDING

....

....

....

YOUR HELP MADE
....
....
....
IT HAPPEN!

To ....

in Recognition of

....

....

....

A Certificate of
Recognition

To ....
for ....
....
....

you
made
the days brighter

....

To ....

for ....

Thank You!

Celebrations

Use celebrations to reward students, staff, and volunteers. Add the finishing touch to a unit or learning venture by having a classroom celebration, or just celebrate a special day. Involve each class member in planning and carrying out these celebrations. Invite families or other classrooms to come to the celebration.

These suggestions are only a small sample of the possible celebrations you can have. For more ideas, go to the library and look at books on parties and celebrations.

Start by making a list.

date .... time .... place ....

decorations ....

activities ....

entertainment ....

food ....

food preparation & service ....

clean up ....

equipment ....

recording the celebration .... video ....
.... film .... written .... tape ....

who to invite

....

....

....

....

....

....

....

invitations ....

thank you notes ....

Special Days for Celebrations

Here is a partial list of special days that you might want to celebrate.

Poetry Day is October 15. Encourage children to write poems for your celebration.

United Nations Day is October 24. Plan a multicultural celebration.

The Sweetest Day falls on the third Saturday in October. Make a card or small gift to give to someone who is ill, aged, or in special need of attention. Make a class trip to a retirement home. Make or assemble a collection of books, games, and toys for a children's home or school.

Pan American Day is April 14. Plan a Latin-American celebration.

For Book Week, hold a bookfair. Have students plan or make large pictures or models of their favorite story-book characters. Honor the student-authors and illustrators. Serve food that is taken from recipes in the students' favorite books. Have the students prepare annotated book lists. Interested students could attend the celebration dressed as a favorite character and read passages from the books they represent.

Forefathers' Day is December 21. This day commemorates the day the Pilgrims landed in Plymouth, Massachusetts. It was first celebrated in 1769 and the following meal was served: whortleberry pudding, succotash, clams, oysters, codfish, seafowl, venison, frostfish, eels, apple pie, cranberry tarts, and cheese. The Pilgrims wore simple clothing.

Have the children prepare a similar meal and follow it with an old twist of a Christmas celebration called Mumming. This tradition comes from England where men and women exchanged costumes on Mumming day—men dressed as women, and women dressed as men. Perform short skits while dressed in these funny costumes.

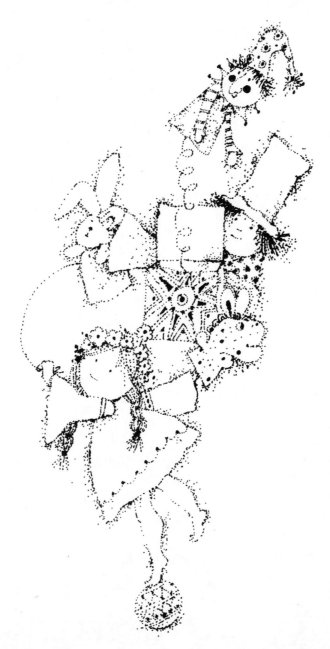

Brotherhood Week is in February, the week of George Washington's birthday. Celebrate the fact that we are all brothers and sisters in the family of man. Turn the classroom into a multicultural celebration with costumes, food, and crafts from each student's heritage.

Make a family-of-man photo exhibit with family photos that each student brings from home. Have the students take pictures of each other and write stories and poems to go with the photographs. Exhibit the photos on small boxes, on large appliance boxes, or on clotheslines strung back and forth in the classroom.

April Fool's Day is April 1. This is a good day to celebrate all the great nonsense that keeps life from getting too serious. Make it a backwards day, dressing and walking backwards. Exchange ridiculous gifts; write silly stories and read them aloud. Hold a joke-telling marathon and a tongue-twister bee (a variation of a spelling bee).

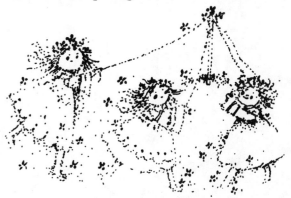

May Day is a spring celebration held on May 1, a wonderful excuse to decorate the room and everyone in it with flowers. Plan a picnic with singing and dancing. Make a traditional maypole, hanging brightly colored ribbons from a flagpole.